D1550231

BEYOND GRAMMAR

BEYOND

An Experience-Based

CSLI PUBLICATIONS

CSLI Lecture Notes Number 88

GRAMMAR

Theory of Language

Rens Bod

Center for the Study of Language and Information • Stanford, California

Copyright © 1998
CSLI Publications
Center for the Study of Language and Information
Leland Stanford Junior University
Printed in the United States
02 01 00 99 98   5 4 3 2 1

Library of Congress Cataloging-in-Publication Data

Bod, Rens, 1965–
Beyond grammar : an experience-based theory of language / Rens Bod.
p.   cm. — (CSLI lecture notes ; no. 88)
Includes bibliographical references.

ISBN 1-57586-151-8 (hardcover : alk. paper).
ISBN 1-57586-150-x (pbk. : alk. paper)

1. Linguistics—Statistical methods. 2. Computational linguistics.
I. Title. II. Series.
P138.5.B63   1998
410′.2′1—DC21   98-26880
CIP

∞ The acid-free paper used in this book meets the minimum requirements of the American National Standard for Information Sciences—Permanence of Paper for Printed Library Materials, ANSI Z39.48-1984.

Longum iter est per praecepta, breve et efficax per exempla.
(Long is the way through rules, short and efficacious through examples.)

    L. Seneca

Es gibt nur die Beispiele.
(There are only examples.)

    L. Wittgenstein

Contents

Preface

During the last few years, a new approach to language processing has started to emerge. This approach, which has become known under the name of "Data Oriented Parsing" or "DOP"[1], embodies the assumption that human language comprehension and production works with representations of concrete past language experiences, rather than with abstract grammatical rules. The models that instantiate this approach therefore maintain corpora of linguistic representations of previously occurring utterances. New utterance-representations are constructed by productively combining (partial) structures from the corpus. A probability model is used to choose from the collection of different structures of different sizes those that make up the most appropriate representation of an utterance.

   In this book, DOP models for various kinds of linguistic representations are described, ranging from tree representations, compositional semantic representations, attribute-value representations, and dialogue representations. These models are studied from formal, linguistic and computational perspectives and are tested on available language corpora. The main outcome of these tests suggests that the productive units of natural language cannot be defined in terms of a minimal set of rules (or constraints or principles), as is usually attempted

---

[1] For examples of work within this framework, see van den Berg et al. (1994), Bod (1991, 92, 93a/b/c/d, 95a/b, 96a/b/c, 98), Bod & Kaplan (1998a/b), Bod & Scha (1994, 96, 97), Bod et al. (1996, 97), Bonnema (1996), Bonnema et al. (1997), Bourigault (1993), Carroll & Weir (1997), Charniak (1996, 1997a), Coleman & Pierrehumbert (1997), Cormons (1998), Goodman (1996, 98), van der Hoeven (1995), Kaplan (1996), Magerman (1993), Rajman (1995a/b), Rajman & Han (1995), Scha (1990, 92), Schaaf (1998), Scholtes (1992a/b, 93), Scholtes & Bloembergen (1992a/b), Schütz (1996), Sekine & Grishman (1995), Sima'an et al. (1994), Sima'an (1995, 96a/b, 97a/b), Tugwell (1995), van Zaanen (1997), Zavrel (1996).

xii / BEYOND GRAMMAR

in linguistic theory, but need to be defined in terms of a redundant set of previously experienced structures with virtually no restriction on their size and complexity. It has been argued that this outcome has important consequences for linguistic theory, leading to an entirely new view of the nature of linguistic competence and the relationship between linguistic theory and models of performance. In particular, it means that the knowledge of a speaker/hearer cannot be understood as a grammar, but as a statistical ensemble of language experiences that changes slightly every time a new utterance is processed.

Although this book may seem primarily intended for readers with a background in computational linguistics, I have given maximal effort to make it comprehensible to all students and researchers of language, from theoretical linguists to psycholinguists and computer scientists. I believe that there is still a cultural gap to be bridged between natural language technology and theory. On the one hand, there is the Statistical Natural Language Processing community which seems to have lost all links with current linguistic theory. On the other hand, there is the Theoretical Linguistics community whose results are often ignored by natural language technology and psycholinguistics. In this book I will argue that there can be no such thing as statistical linguistics without a theory of linguistic representation, and there can be no adequate linguistic theory without a statistical enrichment. If this book helps to bridge the gap between these two communities, its aim has been achieved. On the other hand, I realize that I may be easily criticized by both communities, which is the consequence of being interdisciplinary.

The only background knowledge I assume throughout the book are (1) the basic notions of grammatical theory, such as context-free grammar, Chomsky hierarchy and generative capacity; and (2) the basic notions of probability theory, such as the classical definitions of absolute, conditional and joint probability. Some knowledge of logic and compositional semantics is also helpful. I have tried to keep technical details to a minimum and referred to the relevant literature as much as possible. Having said this, my first aim has been to write a comprehensible book which can be read without the need of external literature.

Some parts of this book rely on previous work published with Remko Scha, Ronald Kaplan, Martin van den Berg, Remko Bonnema and Khalil Sima'an. Some minor parts of chapters 1 and 2 were previously published in Bod & Scha (1996) and Bod & Kaplan (1998b); chapter 8 was partly published in van den Berg, Bod & Scha (1994), while chapter 10 completely relies on Bod & Kaplan (1998b). Some parts from chapter 9 can also be found in Bod (1998) and Bonnema et al. (1997).

This work greatly benefits from discussions I had with many people. I thank Martin van den Berg, Remko Bonnema, Michael Brent, Joan Bresnan, Kenneth Church, John Coleman, Boris Cormons, Walter Daelemans, Mary Dalrymple, Marc Dymetman, Bipin Indurkhya, Mark Johnson, Aravind Joshi, Laszlo Kalman, Martin Kay, Gerard Kempen, Chris Klaassen, Andras Kornai, Steven Krauwer, Willem Levelt, David Magerman, John Maxwell, Fernando Pereira, Stanley Peters, Janet Pierrehumbert, Livia Polanyi, Martin Rajman, Philip Resnik, Mats Rooth, Ivan Sag, Christer Samuelsson, Yves Schabes, Khalil Sima'an, Paul Smolensky, Bangalore Srinivas, Andy Way, Jakub Zavrel, Henk Zeevat, and others I may have forgotten to mention.

I am deeply grateful to Ronald Kaplan and Remko Scha who read previous versions of this work and suggested many valuable improvements. Of course, all remaining errors are my responsibility.

This book could never have been written without the support of NWO, the Netherlands Organization for Scientific Research (Priority Programme Language and Speech Technology).

1

Introduction: what are the productive units of natural language?

One of the most fundamental concepts in modern linguistic theory is the *competence-performance* dichotomy. A linguistic *competence model* aims at characterizing a person's knowledge of a language while a linguistic *performance model* aims at describing the actual production and perception of natural language sentences in concrete situations (Chomsky 1965). This dichotomy has become the methodological paradigm for all formal linguistic theories. It is assumed that the primary goal of linguistics is the development of a theory of language *competence*. Linguistic theory has adopted the formal languages of logic and mathematics as its paradigm examples: a language is viewed as a well-defined infinite set of sentence/meaning pairs that is explicitly characterized by a consistent and non-redundant system of formal rules (a "competence grammar"). It is conjectured that human minds actually employ such rule systems in producing and comprehending new utterances. At the same time, linguistic theory acknowledges explicitly that a competence grammar alone cannot account for all aspects of human language: a person's language *performance* is also influenced by several other mental properties, that do not belong to the core-business of linguistics.

We may illustrate this dichotomy by focussing on one particular performance issue: the problem of disambiguation. As soon as a competence grammar is large enough to cover a non-trivial fragment of a natural language, it assigns to many sentences an extremely large number of alternative syntactic analyses. Human language users, however, tend to perceive only one or two of these. The combinatorial explosion of syntactic analyses (and corresponding semantic interpretations) of natural language sentences has been ignored by linguistic theory, but is well-recognized in psycholinguistics and language technology (cf. Church & Patil 1983; Gibson & Loomis 1994; MacDonald et al. 1994). Martin et al. (1983) list the number of different analyses their grammar assigns to some example sentences:

List the sales of products in 1973	3
List the sales of products produced in 1973	10
List the sales of products in 1973 with the products in 1972	28
List the sales of products produced in 1973 with the products produced in 1972	455

Because of the different attachment possibilities of prepositional phrases and relative clauses, a competence grammar must acknowledge many possible structures for such sentences. Human speakers of English, however, will fail to notice this dazzling degree of ambiguity; not more than a few analyses will spontaneously come to mind. A performance theory of natural language should therefore not be satisfied with describing the space of possible analyses that sentences may get; it should predict which analyses comprehenders actually assign to natural language utterances. Such a performance theory clearly requires non-linguistic knowledge, concerning, for instance, the varying degrees of plausibility of different real-world situations, and the varying occurrence-likelihoods of different words and constructions and their meanings.

It is one of the main goals of this book to show how a statistical enrichment of a linguistic theory can deal with aspects of language performance. In doing so, we will focus on the problem of language disambiguation (although we will also deal with language production and speech recognition). We start by motivating a probabilistic approach to language, after which we deal with the question of what is involved in creating a performance model which can select from all possible analyses of a sentence, the analysis that would be assigned by a natural language user. The resulting model also offers a new view of the nature of linguistic competence and the relationship between linguistic theory and models of performance.

1   A probabilistic approach to language

A long series of psychological investigations indicate that: (1) people register frequencies and differences in frequencies (e.g. Hasher &

Chromiak 1977; Kausler & Puckett 1980; Pearlmutter & MacDonald 1992), (2) analyses that a person has experienced before are preferred to analyses that must be newly constructed (e.g. Hasher & Zacks 1984; Jacoby & Brooks 1984; Bock 1986; Kuiper 1996), and (3) this preference is influenced by the frequency of occurrence of analyses: more frequent analyses are preferred to less frequent ones (e.g. Mehler & Carey 1968; Fenk-Oczlon 1989; Juliano & Tanenhaus 1993; Tanenhaus & Trueswell 1995).

The above statements form an important motivation for a frequency-based approach to a model which aims at characterizing human language performance. The use of probability theory is a straightforward step, since it models the notion of *frequency of occurrence* in a mathematically precise way, offering a coherent and well understood framework. We therefore rewrite the statements (1) through (3) by (4): *a comprehender tends to perceive the most probable analysis of a new utterance on the basis of frequencies of previously perceived utterance-analyses.*

Note that (4) does not say that other possible analyses of an utterance are "wrong". An analysis is formally "correct" if it can be generated by the underlying linguistic theory (the competence model). It is the task of a performance model to select among all correct analyses the analysis which is actually *perceived* by a comprehender. This does not mean that a comprehender is unable to perceive the other analyses of an utterance. He/she has only a very strong tendency towards perceiving a more probable analysis with respect to his/her previous language experiences. What (4) does imply, is, that different linguistic experiences can yield different perceived analyses of utterances. It is interesting to note that there is some support for this implication (Mitchell et al. 1992; Christiansen & MacDonald 1998). However, in the absence of full collections of individual language experiences, we will mostly abstract from these individual differences and limit ourselves to actually available collections of analyzed natural language utterances.

Apart from a psycholinguistic perspective, a statistical approach has also been motivated from an engineering point of view. Statistical extensions of linguistic theories have gained a vast popularity in the field of natural language processing. In this field, it is widely recognized that purely rule-based methods suffer from a lack of robustness in solving uncertainty due to overgeneration (if too many analyses are generated for a sentence) and undergeneration (if no analysis is generated for a sentence). A statistical approach is supposed to be more robust than a purely rule-based approach, since it allows for *a best guess in case of uncertainty* (cf. Garside et al. 1987; Liberman 1991; Liberman & Schabes 1993; Charniak 1993). The success of statistical methods in the field of speech recognition has further reinforced this insight (cf. Church & Mercer 1993).

2 Stochastic grammars and the problem of productive unit size

What does a statistical extension of a linguistic theory, often referred to as a "stochastic grammar", look like? In the literature, we can observe the following recurrent theme: (1) take your favorite linguistic theory (a competence grammar), (2) attach application probabilities to the productive units of this theory. Examples are stochastic context-free grammar (e.g. Suppes 1970; Sampson 1986; Black et al. 1993), stochastic tree-adjoining grammar (Resnik 1992; Schabes 1992), stochastic unification-based grammar (Briscoe & Carroll 1993; Briscoe 1994), stochastic head-driven phrase structure grammar (Brew 1995) and stochastic lexical-functional grammar (Johnson 1996). It would be easy to define, in a similar way, stochastic generalized phrase-structure grammar, stochastic categorial grammar, etc.

A statistically enhanced competence grammar of this sort defines all sentences of a language and all analyses of these sentences. It also assigns probabilities to each of these sentences and each of these analyses. It therefore makes definite predictions about an important class of performance phenomena: the preferences that people display when they choose between different sentences (in language production and speech recognition), or between alternative analyses of sentences (in disambiguation).

The accuracy of these predictions, however, is necessarily limited. Stochastic grammars assume that the statistically significant language units coincide exactly with the linguistic units (rules and lexical items) employed by the competence grammar. The most obvious case of frequency-based bias in human disambiguation behavior therefore falls outside their scope: the tendency to assign previously seen interpretations rather than innovative ones to conventional phrases and other fixed constructions. Idioms, platitudes and conventional phrases demonstrate that constructions of arbitrary size and complexity may be statistically important while they may be completely redundant from a purely linguistic point of view (Bod & Scha 1996). More than that, since larger constructions are usually made up of smaller ones, it is conceptually difficult to decide where to draw the boundaries around a particular set of dependencies (see chapters 3 and 5).

If constructions of arbitrary size and form may be statistically important, which constructions are used in processing and producing new utterances? The language experience of an adult language user consists of a large number of utterance-analyses. Each of these utterance-analyses contains a multitude of constructions: not only the tree of the whole sentence, and all its constituent trees, but also all patterns that can be abstracted from these by introducing "free variables" for lexical elements or complex constituents. Since we do not know beforehand which of these constructions may be important, we should not constrain or predefine the productive language units beforehand, but *take all, arbitrarily large fragments of (previously experienced) utterance-analyses as possible units and let the statistics decide.* This will be the working hypothesis for this book and will be subject to extensive testing.

3 The Data-Oriented Parsing framework: productivity from examples

It is obvious that a given person's past language experience somehow determines the outcome of that person's sentence analysis processes. The basic idea behind the Data-Oriented Parsing or "DOP" approach is that this happens in an essentially direct way. As a representation of a person's past language experience, we use a corpus of previously occurring utterances with their appropriate analyses. Analyses of new utterances are constructed by freely combining fragments from analyses that occur in the corpus. By taking into account the occurrence-frequencies of the fragments, it can be decided which is the most probable analysis that can be constructed in this way.

The DOP approach thus stands in sharp contrast to the usual linguistic approach. As Bod & Kaplan (1998a) observed, a DOP model that incorporates the utterance-representations or analyses of a given linguistic theory does not incorporate the particular grammatical rules and derivational mechanisms of that theory. A DOP model does not even require the identification of a particular collection of larger constructions;

it allows for utterance-analyses to be created from structures of arbitrary size and complexity, even from structures that are actually substructures of other ones. A probability model is used to choose from the collection of different structures of different sizes those that make up the most appropriate analysis of an utterance. Thus, although a DOP model for a given theory of representation will generate (infinitely many) utterance-analyses that are compatible with that theory, it does not depend on or contribute to the discovery of the smallest, non-redundant set of rules for the whole set of utterance-representation assignments.

In accordance with the general DOP architecture outlined by Bod (1995b), a particular DOP model is described by specifying settings for the following four parameters:

(1) a formal definition of a well-formed *representation for utterance-analyses*,

(2) a definition of the *fragments* of the utterance-analyses that may be used as units in constructing an analysis of a new utterance,

(3) a set of *composition operations* by which such fragments may be combined, and

(4) a *probability model* that indicates how the probability of a new utterance-analysis is computed on the basis of the probabilities of the fragments that combine to make it up.

The DOP framework thus allows for a wide range of different instantiations. We hypothesize that human language processing can be modeled as a probabilistic process that operates on a corpus of representations of past language experiences, but we leave open how the utterance-analyses in the corpus are represented, how fragments of these utterance-analyses may be combined, and what the details of the probabilistic calculations are.

In this book, we develop DOP models for several different linguistic representations, ranging from simple phrase-structure trees, compositional semantic representations, attribute-value representations, and dialogue representations. We will study these models from formal, linguistic and computational perspectives, and use them to test the working hypothesis. That is, we will test whether all, arbitrarily large and complex fragments are in fact relevant for predicting the appropriate analysis of a new utterance, or whether we may impose constraints on the fragments, in such a way that the prediction of the appropriate analysis does not deteriorate and perhaps even improves.

A necessary condition for testing a DOP model is the availability of annotated language corpora. Until very recently, the only readily available corpora consisted of syntactically labeled phrase-structure trees, such as the Nijmegen Corpus (van Halteren and Oostdijk 1988), the Lancaster Treebank (Black, Garside and Leech 1993), the Pennsylvania Treebank (Marcus et al. 1993) and the Susanne Corpus (Sampson 1995). The main part of this book therefore deals with simulating the syntactic dimension of language performance. The recent development of corpora with semantic representations (e.g. Bod et al. 1996; Bonnema et al. 1997) allows us to implement DOP models that can simulate semantic interpretation and speech understanding. The comparison of these different DOP models triggers some interesting representation-independent theorems about natural language.

We will see that the DOP framework can incorporate several (psycho)linguistic phenomena that are not directly reflected in the definition of the four parameters. For example, the notion of *recency of occurrence* of language experiences can be incorporated into the fourth parameter of the DOP framework by a probability function which adjusts the frequencies of more recently perceived/produced fragments upwards while the frequencies of less recently perceived/produced fragments are adjusted downwards, possibly down to zero. Thus, although DOP assumes that all (fragments of) language experiences are stored, it does not assume that they are also necessarily remembered: fragments may be forgotten if they are not reinvoked again. We will come back to this in chapter 8.

4 Language comprehension vs. language production

The general DOP architecture suggests a prime interest in language parsing or comprehension. But the framework may just as well be used for language *production*. The problem of production is usually viewed as the reverse of comprehension: given a certain intention or meaning, what is the utterance produced by a language user? Since different utterances may express the same meaning, the goal of a performance model is to select from all possible utterances, the utterance which is actually produced for a given meaning. What holds for comprehension also holds for production: *a language user tends to produce the most probable utterance for a given meaning on the basis of frequencies of previous utterance-representations*. For DOP this means that new utterances are constructed by combining fragments that occur in the corpus, while the frequencies of the fragments are used to determine the most probable utterance for a given meaning.

By allowing fragments of arbitrary size, DOP naturally accounts for the preference language speakers display in using conventional phrases. For example, speakers of English say *What time is it?* rather than *How late is it?*. Although there is no reason to exclude the sentence *How late is it?* from a grammatical point of view, the sentence *What time is it?* is much more frequent in a native speaker's past language experience (given the particular meaning to be conveyed). Both sentences can also be constructed out of smaller fragments, but only *What time is it?* can be constructed out of one simple match. We will see that the DOP probability models exhibit a clear preference for sentences and sentence-analyses that can be constructed out of the largest possible fragments, thus leading to sentences and sentence-analyses that are most similar to previously seen ones (see chapter 2). This preference is particularly important for sentences which are constructed out of *semi*-fixed phrases such as *How old are you?* (vs. *What age do you have?*) or *Are you hungry?* (vs. *Do you have a hunger?*).

The typical case in DOP is that a sentence is partly generated by large fragments (which may be as large as complete corpus analyses) and partly by smaller fragments (which may be as small as simple phrase-structure rules). Moreover, DOP predicts that any fragment can become "conventional", provided that it is perceived or produced often enough. A corpus in DOP is thus not a fixed phrasal lexicon, but a productive ensemble of fragments which is continually updated given new linguistic experience.

The caveats we made about comprehension in section 2 also hold for production: a language user is *not* unable to produce sentences other than the most probable one for a given meaning, but he or she has a very strong tendency towards producing a more likely utterance with respect to his/her previous language experiences. Moreover, DOP conjectures that different linguistic experiences can yield different utterances for expressing the same meaning. It also predicts that a stochastic process gives rise to individual variations in language production: a person does not always say the same thing in the same way.

5 Evaluation of DOP models

Before we go into the details of actual instantiations and implementations of DOP models, we need to say a word about the problem of evaluation. The evaluation of natural language systems has for a long time been a somewhat neglected problem. In the field of natural language parsing, the following procedure has traditionally been used: (1) select a set of test sentences, (2) let the system calculate the "best" analyses for these sentences, and (3) let a native speaker decide whether the "best" analyses are the "appropriate" ones. This procedure has at least one drawback: if a native speaker decides whether an experimentally obtained analysis is "appropriate" (i.e. corresponding to the perceived analysis), he is extremely biased by this analysis. He may judge an analysis as appropriate, while he would have assigned a completely different analysis to this sentence if he had not been confronted by the experimentally generated analysis before. This phenomenon of being influenced by experimental outcomes is well-known; nevertheless, this evaluation procedure is still being used by some parsing systems (e.g. Simmons & Yu 1992; Karlsson et al. 1995).

In order to exclude the influence of experimental outcomes on the appropriateness judgments, it is of utmost importance to establish the appropriate analyses of the test sentences *beforehand* and not afterwards. Moreover, the appropriate analyses should preferably not be established by the experimenter himself, but by a separate annotator. A test procedure which satisfies these demands is known as the *blind testing method*. This method dictates that a manually analyzed language corpus is randomly divided into a training set and a test set. The analyses from the training set may be used to "train" the system, while the sentences of the test set are used as input when the system is tested. The degree to which the most probable analyses generated by the system match with the test set analyses is a measure for the accuracy of the system.

There is a question as to what kind of *accuracy metric* is most adequate to compare the most probable analyses generated by the system with the analyses in the test set. A popular accuracy metric, which has been used to evaluate phrase-structure analyses, is the so-called *bracketing accuracy*. This is defined as the percentage of pairs of brackets of the analyses that are not "crossing" the bracketings in the test set analyses (e.g. Black et al. 1991; Harrison et al. 1991; Pereira and Schabes 1992; Grishman et al. 1992; Schabes et al. 1993; Briscoe 1994).

A reason for the popularity of this metric lies in the fact that it allows for the evaluation of systems that use different phrase-structure grammars. Constituent structures that are formulated in terms of different syntactic categories and different numbers of hierarchical levels, may nevertheless be compared as to their compatibility. (Crossing brackets indicate *in*compatibility.)

We believe that the notion of bracketing accuracy (or any other "partial" accuracy metric, such as *labeled precision/recall*, as used by e.g. Magerman 1995, Collins 1996, Charniak 1997) is too poor for measuring the accuracy of a performance model. In testing a performance model, we are first of all interested in whether the model can correctly select the appropriate analysis from the possible analyses of a test sentence. Therefore we need a metric which demands an exact match between the test result and the test set analysis. We thus define *parse accuracy* as the percentage of the test sentences for which the test result is *identical* to the test set analysis. Although we will also be concerned with a qualitative evaluation of test results, we believe that an accuracy which is based on an *exact match* is most adequate for a quantitative evaluation.

6 Overview of this book

In this chapter, we motivated a probabilistic approach to linguistic characterization from both a psychological and technological point of view. We have given the prerequisites of a DOP model which uses the frequencies of structures in a corpus of experienced utterances-analyses to predict the analyses for new utterances. We have proposed an objective method for evaluating DOP models, which is the blind testing method combined with an exact match accuracy metric.

In the following chapter, we develop a DOP model which is based on simple phrase-structure trees. This model produces and analyzes new utterances by combining subtrees from a corpus. The probabilities of different analyses are estimated on the basis of the occurrence-frequencies of the subtrees involved in their derivations. In chapter 3, we show how this model compares with other probabilistic language models in the context of a Formal Stochastic Language Theory. Next, we deal with the problem of computing the most probable parse of a sentence (chapter 4). In chapter 5, we report on a series of experiments in which we investigate several strategies for restricting the set of corpus subtrees;

it turns out that very few restrictions of this sort are warranted. In chapters 6 and 7, we show how an experience-based model of language can learn new words and structures. In chapter 8, we extend our model to semantic interpretation, and show how discourse and recency can be integrated. In chapter 9, it is studied how DOP can be used for speech and dialogue understanding in the context of a spoken dialogue system. We report on experiments which reinforce the results of chapter 5. In the last chapter, we develop a DOP model for non-context-free representations which account for linguistic phenomena that are not reflected in context-free phrase-structure trees. Finally, we go into the conceptual consequences of our approach, and argue for a new notion of competence and an interestingly different role for linguistic theory.

2

An experience-based model for phrase-structure representations

In this chapter, we give an instantiation of the Data-Oriented Parsing framework which is based on tree structures and which we will call DOP1 (Bod 1992). We make specific choices for each of the relevant components, that is, we specify (1) the representations that are assumed, (2) the fragments of these representations that can be used to generate new representations, (3) the operator that is used to combine fragments, and (4) the probabilistic model that is assumed.

1 Representations

We do not know yet what kind of representations would provide us with the most suitable encoding of a language user's "syntactic structure experience", but the representations employed by current linguistic theories are plausible candidates to consider for this purpose. However, for DOP1 we will stick to a much simpler system: we will encode utterance-analyses as labeled trees, where the labels are primitive symbols. This notation is obviously limited. It does not represent the meanings of constituents; it ignores "deep" or "functional" syntactic structures that do not coincide with surface structures; and it does not even take into account syntactic features such as case, number or gender. We therefore do not expect to stay with this decision for a very long time. But for the moment it has two big advantages: it is very simple, and it is the kind of representation that is used in readily available annotated corpora.

Thus the sentence *John likes Mary* may be assigned a tree such as in figure 2.1. (We have omitted the lexical category N to reduce the number of fragments we have to deal with in the subsequent sections.)

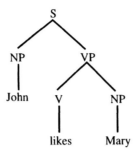

Figure 2.1. A possible analysis tree for *John likes Mary*

2 Fragments

The fragments of the corpus trees that DOP1 uses as units are *subtrees*. A subtree of a tree T is a subgraph t of T such that

(1) t consists of more than one node
(2) t is connected
(3) except for the frontier nodes of t, each node in t has the same daughter nodes as the corresponding node in T

For example, suppose we have the tree T shown in figure 2.1. Then the following trees are valid fragments of T.

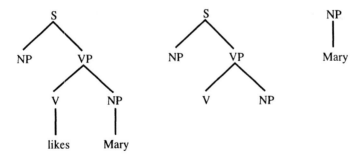

Figure 2.2. Valid fragments of figure 2.1

Note that the definition excludes fragments such as

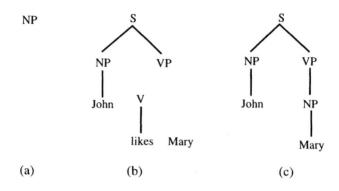

Figure 2.3. Non-valid fragments of figure 2.1

Subtree (a) conflicts with condition (1) which states that a fragment must consist of more than one node. The disconnected subtree (b) conflicts with condition (2). Finally, subtree (c) conflicts with condition (3) which demands that each node in a fragment must have the same daughter nodes as the corresponding node in the tree it is derived from (except for the frontier nodes); this condition has the effect of preserving the integrity of subcategorization dependencies that are typically encoded as sister relations in phrase-structure trees.

Given a corpus of trees C, we define the bag of subtrees of C as the bag in which every subtree occurs exactly as often as it can be identified in a tree in C.

3 Composition operations

DOP1 specifies only one composition operation, a node-substitution operation which is a partial function on pairs of labeled trees; its range is the set of labeled trees. The composition of tree t and tree u, written as $t \circ u$, is defined iff the label on the leftmost nonterminal frontier node of t is identical to the label on the root node of u. If $t \circ u$ is defined, it yields a copy of t in which a copy of u has been substituted on t's leftmost nonterminal frontier node. (The requirement to substitute on the *leftmost* nonterminal makes the composition of two subtrees unique.)

The composition operation is illustrated in figure 2.4 where two fragments from figure 2.1 are combined by leftmost node-substitution:

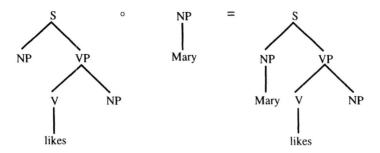

Figure 2.4. Illustration of the composition operation

The resulting tree in 2.4 can be composed with another NP fragment from figure 2.1 to derive an analysis for the sentence *Mary likes John*:

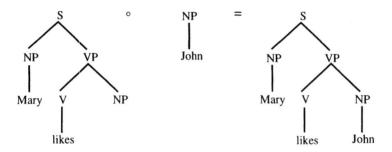

Figure 2.5. Deriving an analysis for *Mary likes John*

In the sequel we will write $(t \circ u) \circ v$ as: $t \circ u \circ v$ with the convention that $\circ$ is *left*-associative.

Given a bag of subtrees B, a sequence of compositions $t_1 \circ \ldots \circ t_n$ with $t_i \in B$ yielding a tree T with root node S and without nonterminal leaves is called a *derivation* of T.

Given a bag of subtrees B, the set of trees with root node S and without nonterminal leaves that can be generated by means of iterative composition of members of B is called the *tree language* generated by B. The set of strings yielded by these trees is called the *string language* generated by B.

Given a corpus of trees C, the tree language generated by the bag of subtrees of the trees of C is said to be the tree language induced by *C*. The string language generated by the bag of subtrees of the trees of *C* is said to be the string language induced by *C*.

4 Probability calculation

By defining a method for extracting subtrees from a corpus and a method for composing such subtrees into new trees, we have effectively established a way to view a corpus as a grammar -- i.e., as a definition of a set of strings with syntactic analyses. This grammar becomes a *stochastic* grammar if we redefine the generation of syntactic trees as a stochastic process that takes the frequency distributions of the corpus subtrees into account: a process that first chooses a subtree at random from among the subtrees with the distinguished root label (for instance S), then composes this subtree with a subtree that is randomly chosen from among the ones that it *can* be composed with, and then repeats that step until a tree results without nonterminal leaves. To every tree and every string we assign the probability that it is generated by this stochastic process.

   Note that this calculation does *not* use the corpus as a sample for estimating the parameter values of a stochastic model of a population. The corpus subtrees are used directly as a stochastic generative system, and new input receives the analysis that is most likely to be generated by that system. (In chapter 7 we will extend this system so as to cope with the problem of learning new words.)

   Before we go into more detail about the computation of probabilities, let us illustrate the stochastic generation process by means of an extremely simple example. Suppose that a corpus of sentence-analyses consists of only the two trees given in figure 2.6.

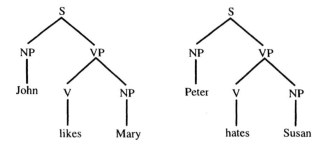

Figure 2.6. A corpus of two trees

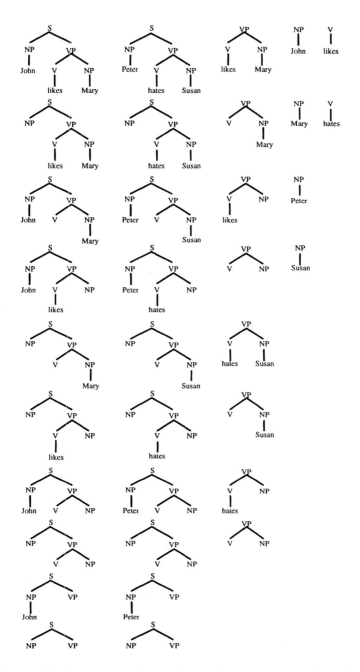

Figure 2.7. The bag of subtrees derived from the trees in figure 2.6

The bag of subtrees extracted from this corpus is represented in figure 2.7. Notice that some subtrees occur twice (a subtree may be extracted from different trees and even several times from a single tree if the same node configuration appears at different positions).

By means of the composition operation, new sentence-analyses can be constructed out of this subtree collection. For instance, an analysis for the sentence *Mary likes Susan* can be generated by combining the following three subtrees from the bag in 2.7:

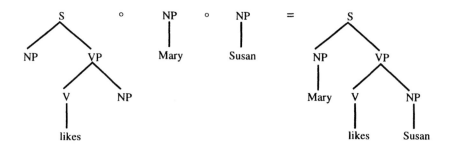

Figure 2.8. Analyzing *Mary likes Susan* by combining subtrees

The probability of this particular derivation is the joint probability of 3 stochastic events:

(1) selecting the subtree S[NP VP[V[likes] NP]] among the sub-
    trees with root label S,
(2) selecting the subtree NP[Mary] among the subtrees with root
    label NP,
(3) selecting the subtree NP[Susan] among the subtrees with root
    label NP.

The probability of each event can be computed by dividing the frequencies of the occurrences of the relevant kinds of subtrees. For instance, the probability of event (1) is computed by dividing the number of occurrences of the subtree S[NP VP[V[likes] NP]] by the total number of occurrences of subtrees with root label S: 1/20.

In general, let | t | be the number of times subtree t occurs in the bag and $r(t)$ be the root node category of t, then the probability assigned to t is

$$P(t) = \frac{|t|}{\sum_{t': r(t')=r(t)} |t'|}$$

Since in our stochastic generation process each subtree selection is independent of the previous selections, the probability of a derivation is the product of the probabilities of the subtrees it involves. Thus, the probability of the derivation in figure 2.8 is: $1/20 \cdot 1/4 \cdot 1/4 = 1/320$. In general, the probability of a derivation $t_1 \circ \ldots \circ t_n$ is given by

$$P(t_1 \circ \ldots \circ t_n) = \prod_i P(t_i)$$

The probability of a parse tree is computed by considering all its derivations. For instance, the parse tree for *Mary likes Susan* derived in figure 2.8 may also be derived as in figure 2.9 or figure 2.10.

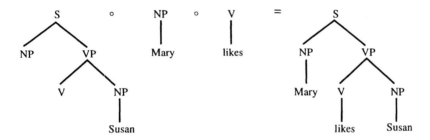

Figure 2.9. A different derivation, yielding the same parse for *Mary likes Susan*

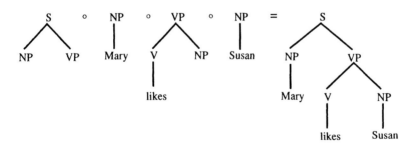

Figure 2.10. One more derivation yielding the same parse for *Mary likes Susan*

Thus, a parse tree can be generated by a large number of different derivations, that involve different fragments from the corpus. Each of these derivations has its own probability of being generated. For instance, the following shows the probabilities of the three example derivations given above.

$$
\begin{array}{llll}
P(\text{figure 2.8}) & = & 1/20 \cdot 1/4 \cdot 1/4 & = & 1/320 \\
P(\text{figure 2.9}) & = & 1/20 \cdot 1/4 \cdot 1/2 & = & 1/160 \\
P(\text{figure 2.10}) & = & 2/20 \cdot 1/4 \cdot 1/8 \cdot 1/4 & = & 1/1280
\end{array}
$$

Table 2.1. Probabilities of the derivations of figures 2.8, 2.9 and 2.10

The probability of a parse tree is the probability that it is produced by any of its derivations. Therefore, the probability of a parse tree T is the sum of the probabilities of its distinct derivations D:

$$P(T) = \Sigma_{D \text{ derives } T} P(D)$$

This step in the calculation usually does not occur when a probabilistically enhanced competence grammar is used. Such grammars aim at identifying exactly one derivation for each syntactic analysis. This makes computations simpler, but restricts the statistical dependencies beforehand. By taking into account all combinations of arbitrarily large corpus-subtrees, no configuration that might possibly be of statistical interest is ignored.

The probability of a parse tree T given that it yields a sentence or word string W is computed by dividing the probability of T by the sum of the probabilities of all parses that yield W:

$$P(T \mid T \text{ yields } W) = \frac{P(T)}{\Sigma_{T' \text{ yields } W} P(T')}$$

Since the sentence *Mary likes Susan* is unambiguous with respect to the corpus, the conditional probability of its parse tree is simply 1, by a vacuous application of the formula above. Of course a larger corpus might contain fragments by which many different representations can be derived for a single sentence, and in that case the above formula for the conditional probability would provide a probabilistic ordering for them.

For instance, suppose the corpus contains the following trees in addition to the trees given in figure 2.6:

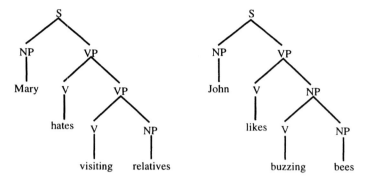

Figure 2.11. Two additional corpus trees

Two different parse trees can then be derived for the sentence *John likes visiting bees*:

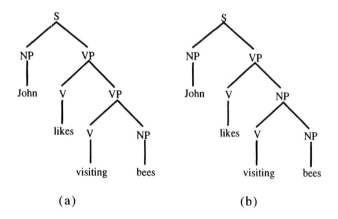

Figure 2.12. Parse trees for *John likes visiting bees*

The DOP1 model will assign a lower probability to the tree 2.12 (a) since the subtree 2.13 (a) of 2.12 (a) is not a corpus fragment and hence must be assembled from several smaller pieces. The subtree 2.13 (b) of 2.12 (b) can also be assembled from smaller pieces, but it also appears twice as a corpus fragment. This means that 2.12 (b) has several more derivations than 2.12 (a), resulting in a relatively higher probability.

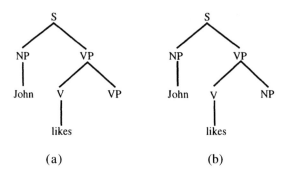

(a)   (b)

Figure 2.13. Two sub-analyses

In general, there tends to be a preference in DOP1 for the parse tree that can be generated by the largest number of derivations. Since a parse tree which can (also) be generated by relatively large fragments has more derivations than a parse tree which can only be generated by relatively small fragments, there is also a preference for the parse tree that can be constructed out of the largest possible corpus fragments, and thus for the parse tree which is most similar to previously seen utterance-analyses.

Notice also that the DOP1 model based on this simple 4-sentence corpus provides analyses for infinitely many sentences. This results from the recursive VP and NP fragments that are produced from the representations in figure 2.11, as illustrated by the sentence *John likes visiting buzzing bees.*

On the other hand, the DOP1 fragment and composition operation definitions limit the range of strings that can be assigned representations. If the corpus contains in addition the following tree

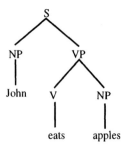

Figure 2.14. An additional corpus tree

then the sentence *John eats* can be assigned no representation. This is because the fragment definition preserves the sister relations in phrase-structure trees; so there is no fragment in the corpus of the form:

Figure 2.15. A fragment which is not in the corpus

and the composition operation (leftmost substitution) is not defined to append new sister nodes. Of course, alternative DOP models with more permissive fragment definitions or more powerful composition operations might provide an analysis for *John eats* on the basis of this corpus.

3

Formal Stochastic Language Theory

In this chapter, we develop a theory in which the properties of stochastic grammars can be formally articulated and compared. We describe DOP1 as a projection of a corpus into a Stochastic Tree-Substitution Grammar (STSG), and we formally compare STSG with other stochastic grammars.

1 A formal language theory of stochastic grammars

The notion of a stochastic grammar usually refers to a finite specification of infinitely many strings with their analyses and probabilities. If we want to compare the formal properties of different stochastic grammars, we need a Formal Stochastic Language Theory. In such a theory, we are not so much concerned with weak and strong generative capacity (as is the case in traditional Formal Language Theory -- e.g. Linz 1990), but with weak and strong *stochastic* generative capacity. The following definitions are therefore convenient.

Definitions

The **stochastic string language** generated by a stochastic grammar G is the set of pairs $<x, P(x)>$ where x is a string from the string language generated by G and $P(x)$ the probability of that string.

The **stochastic tree language** generated by a stochastic grammar G is the set of pairs $<x, P(x)>$ where x is a tree from the tree language generated by G and $P(x)$ the probability of that tree.

In analogy to weak and strong equivalence, we define the following equivalences for stochastic grammars:

Definitions

Two stochastic grammars are called **weakly stochastically equivalent**, iff they generate the same stochastic string language.

Two stochastic grammars are called **strongly stochastically equivalent**, iff they generate the same stochastic tree language.

Note that if two stochastic grammars are weakly stochastically equivalent they are also weakly equivalent (i.e. they generate the same string language). Moreover, if two stochastic grammars are strongly stochastically equivalent they are also strongly equivalent (i.e. they generate the same tree language) and weakly stochastically equivalent.

Now that we have mathematical notions for comparing the generative power of stochastic grammars, we want to exclude the pathological cases of *improper* and *infinitely ambiguous* grammars.

Definition Properness of Grammars

A grammar is called *proper* iff only such nonterminals can be generated whose further rewriting can eventually result in a string of terminals.

Example: Consider the following context free grammar, where S and A are nonterminals and a is a terminal:

$$S \to A$$
$$S \to a$$

This grammar is not proper, since the production $S \to A$ can never result in a string of terminals.

Definition Finite Ambiguity of Grammars

A grammar is called *finitely ambiguous* if there is no finite string that has infinitely many derivations.

Example: The following context free grammar is not finitely ambiguous, since the string a has infinitely many derivations.

$$S \to S$$
$$S \to a$$

Convention: We will only deal with grammars that are proper and finitely ambiguous.

2   DOP1 as a Stochastic Tree-Substitution Grammar

Formally, DOP1 can be viewed as a Stochastic Tree-Substitution Grammar or "STSG" (Bod 1993c). It is useful, therefore, to introduce this formalism.

Definition Stochastic Tree-Substitution Grammar

A *Stochastic Tree-Substitution Grammar* G is a 5-tuple $<V_N, V_T, S, R, P>$ where:

V_N is a finite set of nonterminal symbols.

V_T is a finite set of terminal symbols.

$S \in V_N$ is the distinguished symbol.

R is a finite set of elementary trees whose top nodes and interior nodes are labeled by nonterminal symbols and whose yield nodes are labeled by terminal or nonterminal symbols.

P is a function which assigns to every elementary tree $t \in R$ a probability $P(t)$. For a tree t with a root node symbol $root(t) = \alpha$, $P(t)$ is interpreted as the probability of substituting t on a node α. We require, therefore, that $0 < P(t) \leq 1$ and $\Sigma_{t:root(t)=\alpha} P(t) = 1$.

If t_1 and t_2 are elementary trees such that the leftmost nonterminal frontier node symbol of t_1 is equal to the root node symbol of t_2, then $t_1 \circ t_2$ is the tree that results from substituting t_2 on this leftmost nonterminal frontier node symbol in t_1. The partial function $\circ$ is called *leftmost substitution* or simply *substitution*. We write $(t_1 \circ t_2) \circ t_3$ as $t_1 \circ t_2 \circ t_3$, and in general $(..((t_1 \circ t_2) \circ t_3) \circ ..) \circ t_n$ as $t_1 \circ t_2 \circ t_3 \circ ... \circ t_n$.

A *leftmost derivation* generated by an STSG G is a tuple of elementary trees $<t_1,...,t_n>$ such that $t_1,...,t_n$ are elements of R, the root node of t_1 is labeled by S and the frontier of $t_1 \circ ... \circ t_n$ is labeled by terminal symbols. The set of leftmost derivations generated by G is thus given by

Derivations(G) =

$$\{<t_1,...,t_n> \mid t_1,...,t_n \in R \wedge root(t_1) = S \wedge frontier(t_1 \circ ... \circ t_n) \in V_T^+\}$$

For convenience we will use the term *derivation* for leftmost derivation. A derivation $<t_1,...,t_n>$ is called a derivation of tree T, iff $t_1 \circ ... \circ t_n = T$. A derivation $<t_1,...,t_n>$ is called a derivation of word string W, iff $frontier(t_1 \circ ... \circ t_n) = W$. The probability of a derivation $<t_1,...,t_n>$ is defined as the product of the probabilities of the elementary trees it consists of.

A *parse tree* generated by an STSG G is a tree T such that there is a derivation $<t_1,...,t_n> \in Derivations(G)$ for which $t_1 \circ ... \circ t_n = T$. The set of parse trees, or *tree language*, generated by G is given by

$$Parses(G) = \{T \mid \exists <t_1,...,t_n> \in Derivations(G) : t_1 \circ ... \circ t_n = T\}$$

For reasons of conciseness we will often use the terms *parse* or *tree* for a parse tree. A parse whose yield is equal to string W, is called a parse of W. The probability of a parse is defined as the sum of the probabilities of its distinct derivations.

A *word string* generated by an STSG G is an element of V_T^+ such that there is a parse generated by G whose yield is equal to the word string. For convenience we will often use the term *string* instead of word string. The set of strings, or *string language*, generated by G is given by

$$Strings(G) = \{W \mid \exists T : T \in Parses(G) \land W = frontier(T)\}$$

The probability of a string is defined as the sum of the probabilities of its distinct parses. The probability of a string is thus also equal to the sum of the probabilities of its derivations.

It is evident that DOP1 is an instantiation of STSG. DOP1 projects a corpus of tree structures into an STSG, where the subtrees of DOP1 are the elementary trees of the STSG, and the corpus probabilities of the subtrees of DOP1 are the probabilities of the corresponding elementary trees of the STSG.

3 A comparison between Stochastic Tree-Substitution Grammar and Stochastic Context-Free Grammar

The oldest of all stochastic enrichments of context-free languages is the so-called Stochastic Context-Free Grammar or SCFG (Booth 1969; Suppes 1970). An SCFG enriches each rewrite rule of a CFG with a probability that corresponds to the application probability of this rule. The stochastic dependencies captured by SCFG are thus limited to the scope of single rewrite rules. It may be clear that SCFGs run into trouble if faced with solving ambiguities that go beyond the scope of single rewrite rules. It is therefore almost evident that SCFGs are stochastically weaker than STSGs. However, as an example of how Formal Stochastic Language Theory may be used to formally articulate this, we will compare SCFG and STSG in the context of this theory. Let us start with the definition of SCFG.[2]

Definition Stochastic Context-Free Grammar

A *Stochastic Context-Free Grammar G* is a 5-tuple $<V_N, V_T, S, R, P>$ where:

V_N is a finite set of nonterminal symbols.

V_T is a finite set of terminal symbols.

$S \in V_N$ is the distinguished symbol.

R is a finite set of productions each of which is of the form $\alpha \rightarrow \beta$, where $\alpha \in V_N$ and $\beta \in (V_N \cup V_T)^+$.

P is a function which assigns to every production $\alpha \rightarrow \beta \in R$ a probability $P(\alpha \rightarrow \beta)$, for which holds that $0 < P(\alpha \rightarrow \beta) \leq 1$ and $\Sigma_x P(\alpha \rightarrow x) = 1$.

The probability of a leftmost derivation (and its corresponding parse tree) generated by an SCFG is equal to the product of the probabilities associated with the productions applied. Note that, contrary to STSG, every parse tree is generated by exactly one leftmost derivation. The probability of a string generated by an SCFG is equal to the sum of the probabilities of all its derivations.

We will now compare STSG with SCFG in terms of respectively weak and strong stochastic equivalence.

Proposition 1
For every STSG there exists a weakly stochastically equivalent SCFG.

---

[2] This definition follows Booth (1969), Fu (1974), Levelt (1974), Wetherell (1980), Fujisaki et al. (1989) and Jelinek et al. (1990).

Proof of Proposition 1

Given an STSG G, we convert every elementary tree $t \in R$ into a context-free production $root(t) \rightarrow frontier(t)$. This may lead to multiple occurrences of the same production, since different elementary trees may have the same root and frontier. To every such production a probability is assigned which is equal to the probability of the elementary tree from which the production is derived. In order to eliminate multiple occurrences of productions, we collapse equivalent productions and add up their probabilities. The resulting SCFG G' generates the same string language as G. It is easy to see that the sum of the probabilities of all derivations of a string in G is equal to the sum of the probabilities of all derivations of this string in G'. This means that G and G' assign the same probability to every string in their string language. Thus, G and G' are weakly stochastically equivalent.

□

Proposition 2

For every SCFG there exists a weakly stochastically equivalent STSG.

Proof of Proposition 2

Given an SCFG G, we convert every production $\alpha \rightarrow \beta \in R$ into a unique elementary tree t of depth 1 such that $root(t) = \alpha$ and $frontier(t) = \beta$. Every such tree is assigned a probability which is equal to the probability of the production from which the tree is derived. The resulting STSG G' generates the same string language and tree language as G. It is easy to see that for every derivation in G there is a unique derivation in G' with the same probability. Thus, the sum of the probabilities of all derivations of a string in G is equal to the sum of the probabilities of all derivations of this string in G'. This means that G and G' assign the same probability to every string in their string language. Thus, G and G' are weakly stochastically equivalent.

□

From the propositions 1 and 2 the following corollary can be deduced.

Corollary 1

The set of stochastic string languages generated by STSGs is equal to the set of stochastic string languages generated by SCFGs.

Corollary 1 is significant in the sense that if we were only interested in the strings and not in the trees (for instance for the task of string prediction in speech recognition output), we can convert an STSG (and thus a DOP1 model) into a more succinct SCFG.

Proposition 3
For every SCFG there exists a strongly stochastically equivalent STSG.

Proof of Proposition 3
Consider the proof of proposition 2. Since G and G' generate the same tree language and every derivation in G corresponds to a unique derivation in G' with the same probability, G and G' are strongly stochastically equivalent.

□

Proposition 4
There exists an STSG for which there is no strongly equivalent SCFG.

Proof of Proposition 4
Consider the following STSG G consisting of one elementary tree with a probability equal to 1:

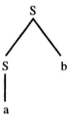

Figure 3.1. An STSG consisting of one elementary tree

The tree language generated by G is equal to the set containing only the above elementary tree. An SCFG is strongly equivalent with G if it generates only the above tree. An SCFG which generates the above tree should contain the productions $S \rightarrow S\ b$ and $S \rightarrow a$. But such an SCFG generates more trees than just the above tree. Contradiction.

□

Proposition 5
There exists an STSG for which there is no strongly stochastically equivalent SCFG.

Proof of Proposition 5
Consider the proof of proposition 4. Since strong stochastic equivalence implies strong equivalence, there is no SCFG which is strongly stochastically equivalent with G.

□

From the propositions 3 and 5 the following corollary can be deduced.

Corollary 2
The set of stochastic tree languages generated by SCFGs is a proper subset of the set of stochastic tree languages generated by STSGs.

Though corollary 2 may seem a significant result, it mainly follows from the property that STSGs are not always strongly equivalent with SCFGs. In the context of stochastic language theory, however, we are not so much interested in tree languages as in *stochastic* tree languages. Thus, it is more interesting to compare stochastic tree languages of *strongly equivalent grammars*.

Proposition 6
There exists an STSG for which there is a strongly equivalent SCFG but no strongly stochastically equivalent SCFG.

Proof of Proposition 6
Consider the STSG G in figure 3.2 consisting of three elementary trees that are all assigned with a probability of 1/3.[3] The string language generated by G is $\{ab^*\}$. Thus the only (proper) SCFG G' which is strongly equivalent with G consists of the following productions:

$$S \rightarrow S\,b \qquad (1)$$
$$S \rightarrow a \qquad (2)$$

---

[3] This STSG is also interesting because it can be projected from a DOP1 model whose corpus of sentence-analyses consists only of tree t_1.

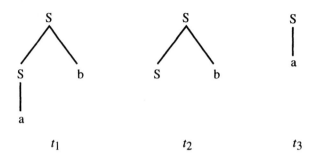

Figure 3.2. An STSG consisting of three elementary trees

G' is strongly stochastically equivalent with G iff it assigns the same probabilities to the parse trees in the tree language as assigned by G. Let us consider the probabilities of two trees generated by G, i.e. the trees represented by t_1 and t_3.[4] The tree represented by t_3 has exactly one derivation, which consists of the elementary tree t_3. The probability of generating this tree is hence equal to 1/3. The tree represented by t_1 has two derivations: by selecting elementary tree t_1, or by combining the elementary trees t_2 and t_3. The probability of generating this tree is equal to the sum of the probabilities of its two derivations, which is equal to 1/3 + 1/3 · 1/3 = 4/9.

If G' is strongly stochastically equivalent with G, it should assign the probabilities 4/9 and 1/3 to the trees represented by t_1 and t_3 respectively. The tree t_3 is exhaustively generated by production (2); thus the probability of this production should be equal to 1/3: $P(S{\rightarrow}a) = 1/3$. The tree t_1 is exhaustively generated by applying productions (1) and (2); thus the product of the probabilities of these productions should be equal to 4/9: $P(S{\rightarrow}Sb) \cdot P(S{\rightarrow}a) = 4/9$. By substitution we get: $P(S{\rightarrow}Sb) \cdot 1/3 = 4/9$, which implies that $P(S{\rightarrow}Sb) = 4/3$. This means that the probability of the production $S{\rightarrow}Sb$ should be larger than 1, which is not allowed. Thus, G' cannot be made strongly stochastically equivalent with G.

□

---

[4] Note that the trees t_1 and t_3 are both elements of the set of (elementary) trees R of G and of the tree language generated by G.

The (proof of) proposition 6 is an important result since it shows that STSGs are not only stronger than SCFGs because there are STSGs for which there are no strongly equivalent SCFGs, but that STSGs are really *stochastically* stronger, also with respect to SCFGs that are strongly equivalent to STSGs. It also makes clear why STSGs are more powerful: STSGs can attach probabilities to structures larger than singular rewrite rules, while SCFGs cannot. One may propose to make the probabilities of rewrite rules in SCFG conditional on other rewrite rules. This will be the topic of the next section.

4 Other stochastic grammars

In this section, we informally compare STSG with other stochastic grammars: Stochastic History-Based Grammar, Stochastic Lexicalized Tree-Adjoining Grammar, and some other stochastic lexicalized grammars. These grammars have been proposed to overcome the stochastic context-insensitiveness of SCFG.

4.1 Stochastic History-Based Grammar (SHBG)

Stochastic History-Based Grammars (SHBG[5]) are developed by Black et al. (1993a/b), though introduced earlier by Smith (1973). In SHBG, the probability of applying a rewrite rule in a leftmost derivation is made conditional on the rules that were used before in that derivation. In Black et al. (1993b: 31), it is said that SHBG provides "a very rich if not the richest model of context ever attempted in a probabilistic parsing model". However, the limitation to a leftmost derivation for conditionalizing the probability of a rule means that still not all possible stochastic dependencies are captured.

Let us illustrate this with the sentence *The emaciated man starved*, of which an analysis is given in figure 3.3. The numbers in the figure refer to the order of applications of the rules r_i in a leftmost derivation of this sentence. Thus the first rule r_1 corresponds to $S \rightarrow NP\ VP$; the second rule, r_2, to $NP \rightarrow Det\ Nbar$, etc.

---

[5] My abbreviation.

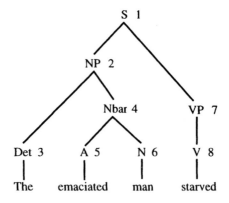

Figure 3.3. Analysis of the sentence *The emaciated man starved* with rule ordering.

Suppose that there is a stochastic dependency between the words *emaciated* and *starved* which is independent of the words *The* and *man*. An adequate stochastic grammar should be able to account for this specific dependency between *emaciated* and *starved*. It turns out that SHBG is not able to do so. To show this, let us explain with somewhat more detail the probabilistic background of SHBG. Assume that the probability of rule r_1 in figure 3.3 (i.e. $S \rightarrow NP\ VP$) is given by $P(r_1)$. Then, since in SHBG the rule probability is made conditional on the former rules in the leftmost derivation, the conditional probability of rule r_2 is given by $P(r_2 \mid r_1)$. The conditional probability of r_3 is given by $P(r_3 \mid r_2, r_1)$ and so forth. The probability of the whole analysis is equal to the product of the conditional probabilities of the rules: $P(r_1) \cdot P(r_2 \mid r_1) \cdot P(r_3 \mid r_2, r_1) \cdot \ldots \cdot P(r_8 \mid r_7, r_6, r_5, r_4, r_3, r_2, r_1)$. In general, the probability of an analysis in SHBG generated by a leftmost derivation $r_1, r_2, \ldots, r_n$ is given by $\Pi_i\ P(r_i \mid r_{i-1}, r_{i-2} \ldots r_1)$ (Black et al. 1993a: 205).

We thus note that SHBG can capture a dependency between all lexical items *The, emaciated, man* and *starved* (and their structure). But there is no way for SHBG to account for the specific dependency between *emaciated* and *starved*, without *the* and *man*. What would be needed are conditional rule probabilities such as $P(r_8 \mid r_7, r_5, r_4, r_2, r_1)$ where the probability of r_8 is made conditional on all former rules except on r_6 and r_3. The definition of SHBG does not account for such probabilities, due to the restriction to a leftmost derivation for conditionalizing the probabilities of rewrite rules (and the sequence r_1, r_2, r_4, r_5, r_7, r_8 does not correspond to a leftmost derivation). Even if a so-called "finite Markov history" is used, SHBG can still only describe structural relations between items like *starved* and *man*, *emaciated* and *man*, or *emaciated*, *man* and *starved*, but not between *emaciated* and *starved* alone, since *man* is produced after *emaciated* and before *starved* in a leftmost derivation. Moreover, any modification of SHBG to another canonical derivation (rightmost, leftcorner etc.) would yield analogous limitations.

In STSG, on the other hand, the dependency between *emaciated* and *starved* can be captured by an elementary tree in which *emaciated* and *starved* are the only lexical items, and where *the* and *man* are left out, as is shown in figure 3.4.

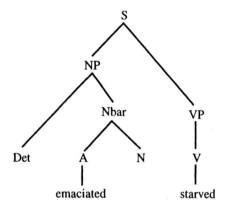

Figure 3.4. Elementary tree with *emaciated* and *starved*.

The above example is somewhat artificial and displays a dependency which is strongly semantic in nature. An example which expresses a more syntactic kind of dependency, is illustrated by the following sentence from the Air Travel Information System (ATIS) corpus (Hemphill et al., 1990): *Show me flights from Dallas to Atlanta.* In the ATIS corpus, the NP-construction *flights from ... to ...* occurs extremely frequently and is almost idiomatic.

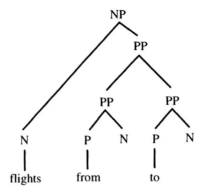

Figure 3.5. Elementary tree corresponding to the construction
flights from ... to ... .

It may be clear that, analogous to the previous example, SHBG can compute a probability for the specific NP-construction *flights from Dallas to Atlanta*, but it cannot compute a probability for the more general NP-construction where *Dallas* and *Atlanta* are left out (figure 3.5). This is a serious shortcoming, since for the correct disambiguation of a new sentence which contains an NP-construction like *flights from ... to ...*, it may be important to describe this general construction as one statistical unit. STSG, on the other hand, can easily describe this NP as a statistical unit by simply attaching a probability to this construction. The same limitations of SHBG occur with dependencies between words like *nearest* and *to* in the ATIS NP-construction *the nearest airport to Dallas*.

4.2 Stochastic Lexicalized Tree-Adjoining Grammar (SLTAG)
Although SLTAG (Resnik 1992; Schabes 1992) is not a stochastic enrichment of a context-free grammar, but of a tree-adjoining grammar belonging to the class of mildly context-sensitive grammars (Joshi 1987; Joshi et al. 1991), it is interesting to deal with SLTAG because of its similarity with STSG. A stochastic lexicalized tree-adjoining grammar assigns a probability to each lexicalized elementary (*initial* or *auxiliary*) tree that corresponds to the probability that this elementary tree is combined either by substitution or adjunction with another elementary tree. If we leave out the adjunction operation, SLTAG is formally equivalent with STSG. In principle, SLTAG can thus capture at least the

stochastic dependencies that can be captured by STSG. However, if we look at current instantiations of SLTAG, we find two shortcomings:

1. Since SLTAG is linguistically motivated by tree-adjoining grammar, there are constraints on the form and use of elementary trees. For instance, modifiers are usually represented by separate auxiliary trees, which means that in analyzing the sentence *The emaciated man starved*, the modifier *emaciated* is inserted in the NP *the man* by means of adjunction. Linguistically this may be elegant, but statistically the dependency between *emaciated* and *starved* is lost, since they are not allowed to appear in a single elementary tree. The same happens with the dependency between the words *nearest* and *to* in the ATIS sentence *Show the nearest airport to Dallas*.

2. Current implementations of SLTAG only take into account the probability of a derivation (cf. Resnik 1992; Schabes 1992), and not the probability of a resulting tree (so-called "derived tree"). This seems statistically suboptimal, since, like in STSG, the probability of a derivation is different from the probability of a tree (see Schabes & Waters 1996).

Thus, current instantiations of SLTAG are based on the assumption that the statistical dependencies coincide with the linguistic dependencies of the underlying competence model. To create an adequate performance model based on TAG, we believe that is not sufficient to attach probabilities to the competence units of this model. Instead, the productive units may correspond to arbitrarily large trees from a corpus of analyzed language utterances (see chapter 5).

4.3 Other stochastic lexicalized grammars

Another, more recent tradition of stochastic grammars extends SCFGs to statistical relations between constituent head words. This is accomplished by associating each nonterminal in a parse tree with the head word of the underlying constituent (e.g. Collins 1996, 1997; Eisner 1996, 1997; Charniak 1997b). Although such head-based stochastic lexicalized grammars are richer than simple SCFGs, they are still limited in that they do not cover dependencies that involve *non-head* words.

Consider again the sentence *Show the nearest airport to Dallas*, where the prepositional phrase *to Dallas* can be attached either to the verb *Show* or to the noun *airport*. In head-based stochastic lexicalized grammars, the probability with which the PP-head *to* occurs with the VP-head *Show* is contrasted with the probability with which the PP-head *to* occurs with the NP-head *airport*. However, the appropriate PP-attachment does depend neither on *Show* nor on *airport*, but on the modifier *nearest* which is not a head of either of the two constituents.

Thus, there can be significant dependencies that go beyond the statistical relations between constituent head words. STSG can capture these dependencies by an elementary tree in which *nearest* and *to* are the only lexical items (figure 3.6).

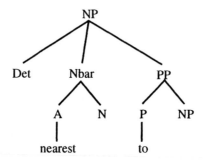

Figure 3.6. Elementary tree with a non-head word

Note that dependencies involving non-head words are much more common than one might think at first hand, e.g. in constructions like *An obvious rule to everybody, John has a faster computer than Peter, Smoke an occasional cigarette*, etc.

5 Open questions

There are still several problems to be solved regarding the relations between stochastic grammars. So far, we have only designed the contours of a Formal Stochastic Language Theory which allowed us to formally compare STSG with SCFG. We believe that the following open questions need also to be treated within such a theory (whose solutions fall beyond the scope of this book).

- Is there a stochastic enrichment of CFG which is stochastically stronger than STSG? We haven't found one yet. It is, for instance, easy to show that a history-based version of STSG yields again an STSG.

- Is there a stochastic hierarchy within the class of stochastic enrichments of CFGs, where SCFG is at the bottom, STSG at the top, and SHBG somewhere in between?

- If the former question can be answered positively, are there similar stochastic hierarchies in the other classes of the Chomsky hierarchy?

4

Parsing and disambiguation

Before we can test DOP1 on actual language corpora, we must deal with the problem of computing the most probable parse of a sentence. For conceptual reasons, we will distinguish between parsing and disambiguation. By parsing we mean generating a parse forest for an input sentence. By disambiguation we mean the selection of the most probable parse from this forest. The algorithms we discuss do not exploit the particular properties of DOP1; it works with any Stochastic Tree-Substitution Grammar.

1 Parsing

For the generation of a parse forest for an input sentence, we can use algorithms that exist for context-free grammars, which parse an input sentence of n words with a time complexity which is polynomial (usually cubic) in n. These parsers make use of a chart or well-formed substring table. They take as input a set of context-free rewrite rules and a sentence and produce as output a chart of labeled phrases. A labeled phrase is a sequence of words labeled with a category symbol which denotes the syntactic category of that phrase. A chart-like parse forest can be obtained by including pointers from a category to the other categories which caused it to be placed in the chart. Algorithms that accomplish this can be found in e.g. Kay (1980), Winograd (1983), Jelinek et al. (1990), Stolcke (1995).

The chart parsing approach can be applied to parsing with Stochastic Tree-Substitution Grammars if we note that every elementary tree t can be viewed as a context-free rewrite rule: $root(t) \rightarrow frontier(t)$. For instance, the elementary tree in figure 4.1 can be viewed as the rule $PP \rightarrow from N to N$.

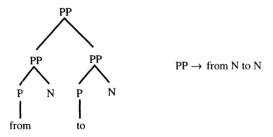

PP → from N to N

Figure 4.1. An elementary tree can be viewed as a rewrite rule

In order to preserve the internal structure of an elementary tree, we must also remember for every converted rule its original elementary tree (together with its probability). This can, for instance, be accomplished by labeling the phrases of the chart not just by their corresponding syntactic categories but by their full elementary trees and probabilities. Note that in a chart-like forest generated by an STSG, different derivations that generate identical trees do not collapse. We will therefore talk about a *derivation forest* generated by an STSG (cf. Sima'an et al. 1994).

The following formal example illustrates what such a derivation forest may look like. In the example, we leave out the probabilities of the elementary trees, that will be needed only in the disambiguation phase. The visual representation is based on Kay (1980): every entry (i,j) in the chart is indicated by an edge and spans the words between the ith and the jth position of a sentence. Every edge is labeled with linked elementary trees that constitute subderivations of the underlying subsentence. The set of elementary trees of the example STSG consists of the trees in figure 4.2.

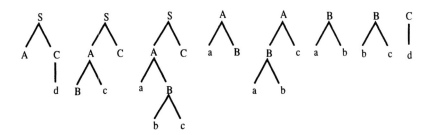

Figure 4.2. Elementary trees of an example STSG

For the input string **abcd**, this gives the derivation forest in figure 4.3.

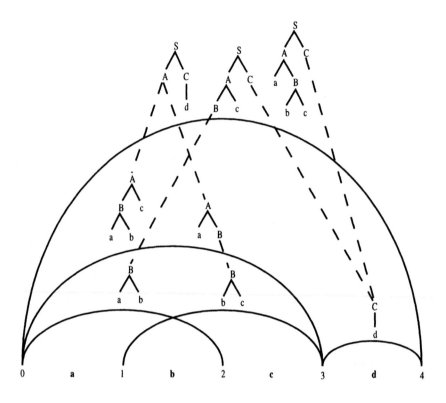

Figure 4.3. Derivation forest for the string **abcd**

Note that some of the derivations in the forest generate the same tree. By exhaustively unpacking the forest, four different derivations generating two different trees are obtained. Both trees are generated twice, by different derivations (with possibly different probabilities). We may raise the question as to whether we can pack the forest by collapsing spurious derivations, summing up their probabilities. Unfortunately, no efficient procedure is known that accomplishes this (note that there can be exponentially many derivations for one tree and there can be exponentially many trees for one string). Sima'an (1995) and Goodman (1996) give some optimizations for generating derivation forests, but their methods still yield spurious forests in that different derivations may yield the same tree. This means that one must still sum over several derivations for each parse tree (Goodman 1996:147; Bod 1996a).

2 Disambiguation

Polynomial time parsing does not guarantee polynomial time disambiguation. A sentence may have exponentially many parse trees and any such tree may have exponentially many derivations. Therefore, in order to find the most probable parse of a sentence, it is not efficient to compare the probabilities of the parses by exhaustively unpacking the chart. Even for determining the probability of one parse, it is not efficient to add the probabilities of all derivations of that parse.

2.1 Viterbi optimization is not applicable to finding the most probable parse

When parsing on the basis of an SCFG (stochastic context-free grammar) or an STSG, the most probable derivation of a sentence can be selected in cubic time by means of a procedure known as Viterbi optimization (Viterbi 1967; Fujisaki et al. 1989; Jelinek et al. 1990). When an SCFG is used, the most probable derivation also generates the most probable parse (since every parse is generated by exactly one derivation). But when an STSG is used, this is not the case -- since the probability of a parse is the sum of the probabilities of all its different derivations.

Let us look in more detail at the Viterbi optimization algorithm. The basic idea of Viterbi is the elimination of low probability subderivations in a bottom-up fashion. Two different subderivations of the same part of the sentence whose resulting subparses have the same root can both be developed (if at all) to derivations of the whole sentence in the same ways. Therefore, if one of these two subderivations has a lower probability, it can be eliminated. This is illustrated by a formal example in figure 4.4. Suppose that during bottom-up parsing of the string *abcd* two subderivations *d1* and *d2* have been generated for the substring *abc*, with the following subparses:

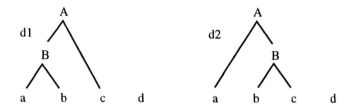

Figure 4.4. Two subderivations *d1* and *d2* for the substring *abc*

If the probability of *d1* is higher than the probability of *d2*, we can eliminate *d2* if we are interested in finding the most probable <u>derivation</u> of *abcd*. But if we are interested in finding the most probable <u>parse</u> of *abcd* (generated by an STSG), we are not allowed to eliminate *d2*. This can be seen by the following. Suppose that we have the additional elementary tree given in figure 4.5.

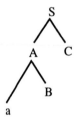

Figure 4.5. Additional elementary tree

This elementary tree may be developed to a tree that can also be developed by *d2*, but not to a tree that can be developed by *d1*. And since the probability of a parse tree is equal to the sum of the probabilities of all its derivations, it is still possible that *d2* contributes to the generation of the most probable parse. Therefore we are not allowed to eliminate *d2*.

This counter-example does not prove that there is no optimization that allows for polynomial time selection of the most probable parse, but it makes clear that a *best-first* search, as accomplished by Viterbi, is not adequate for finding the most probable parse in STSG. In the past few years, several researchers have tried to find optimizations. But the algorithms that were found either turned out to be still exponential (Sima'an et al. 1994), or did not refer to the most probable parse

(Goodman 1996). Finally, Sima'an (1996b) proved that there is no deterministic polynomial time algorithm for finding the most probable parse of a sentence in STSG (i.e., the problem of computing the most probable parse in STSG is NP-hard).

We should of course ask how often the most probable derivation in fact happens to yield the most probable parse. The experimental results we discuss in chapter 5, however, indicate that calculating the most probable parse is indeed more accurate than choosing the parse generated by the most probable derivation.

2.2 Monte Carlo disambiguation: estimating the most probable parse by sampling random derivations

Although there is no deterministic polynomial algorithm for finding the most probable parse, there may be an algorithm that *estimates* a most probable parse with an error that can be made arbitrarily small. We now consider this possibility.

We have seen that a best-first search, as accomplished by Viterbi, can be used for finding the most probable derivation in STSG but not for finding the most probable parse. If we apply instead of a best-first search, a *random-first* search, we can generate a random derivation from the derivation forest -- provided that the random choices are based on the probabilities of the subderivations. By iteratively generating a large number of random derivations we can estimate the most probable parse as the parse which results most often from these random derivations (since the probability of a parse is the probability that any of its derivations occurs). The most probable parse can be estimated as accurately as desired by making the number of random samples sufficiently large. According to the Law of Large Numbers, the most often generated parse converges to the most probable parse. Methods that estimate the probability of an event by taking random samples are known as Monte Carlo methods (Meyer 1956; Hammersley & Handscomb 1964; Motwani & Raghavan 1995).

The selection of a random derivation can be accomplished in a bottom-up fashion analogous to Viterbi. Instead of selecting the most probable subderivation at each node-sharing in the chart, a random subderivation is selected at each node-sharing (in such a way that a subderivation that has m times as large a probability as another subderivation also has m times as large a chance to be chosen as this other subderivation). Once arrived at the S-node, the random derivation of the whole sentence can be retrieved by tracing back the choices made at each node-sharing. We may of course postpone sampling until the S-node, such that we sample directly from the distribution of all S-derivations. But this would take exponential time, since there may be exponentially many derivations for the whole sentence. By sampling bottom-up at every node where ambiguity appears, the maximum number of different subderivations at each node-sharing is bounded to a constant (the total number of rules of that node), and therefore the time complexity of generating a random derivation of an input sentence is equal to the time complexity of finding the most probable derivation, i.e. linear in grammar size G and cubic in sentence length n: $O(Gn^3)$. This is exemplified by the following algorithm, which was originally published in Bod (1995b).

Algorithm 1: Sampling a random derivation in $O(Gn^3)$ time

Given a derivation forest of a sentence of n words, consisting of labeled entries (i,j) that span the words between the ith and the jth position of the sentence. Every entry is labeled with elementary trees, together with their probabilities, that define the last step in a set of subderivations of the underlying subsentence. Sampling a derivation from the chart consists of choosing at random one of the elementary trees for every root-node at every labeled entry (bottom-up, breadth-first)[6]:

for *length* := 1 **to** n **do**
    for *start* := 0 **to** n − *length* **do**
        for chart-entry *(start, start + length)* **do**
            for each root node *X* **do**
                select at random an elementary tree with root node *X*;
                eliminate the other elementary trees with root node *X*;

Let { (e_1, p_1) , (e_2, p_2) , ... , (e_n, p_n) } be a probability distribution of events e_1, e_2, ..., e_n; an event e_i is said to be *randomly selected* iff its chance of being selected is equal to p_i. In order to allow for "simple sampling" (Cochran 1963), where every event has an equal chance of

---

[6] The heuristics of sampling bottom-up, breadth-first can be changed into any other order (e.g.: top-down, depth-first). We chose the current algorithm for its analogy with Viterbi optimization algorithms for SCFGs (cf. Jelinek et al. 1990).

being selected, one may convert a probability distribution into a sample space such that the frequency of occurrence r_i of each event e_i is a positive integer equal to $s \cdot p_i$, where s is the size of the sample space.

We thus have an algorithm that selects a random derivation from a derivation forest. The parse tree that results from this derivation constitutes a first guess for the most probable parse. A more reliable guess can be computed by sampling a larger number of random derivations, and selecting the parse which results most often from these derivations. How large a sample set should be chosen?

Let us first consider the probability of error: the probability that the parse that is most frequently generated by the sampled derivations, is in fact not equal to the most probable parse. An upper bound for this probability is given by $\sum_{i \neq 0} (1 - (\sqrt{p_0} - \sqrt{p_i})^2)^N$, where the different values of i are indices corresponding to the different parses, 0 is the index of the most probable parse, p_i is the probability of parse i; and N is the number of derivations that was sampled (cf. Hammersley & Handscomb 1964; Deming 1966).

This upper bound on the probability of error becomes small if we increase N, but if there is an i with p_i close to p_0 (i.e., if there are different parses in the top of the sampling distribution that are almost equally likely), we must make N very large to achieve this effect. If there is no unique most probable parse, the sampling process will of course not converge on one outcome. In that case, we are interested in all of the parses that outrank all the other ones. But also when the probabilities of the most likely parses are very close together without being exactly equal, we may be interested not in *the* most probable parse, but in the set of all these almost equally highly probable parses. This reflects the situation in which there is an ambiguity which cannot be resolved by probabilistic syntactic considerations.

We conclude, therefore, that the task of a syntactic disambiguation component is the calculation of the probability distribution of the various possible parses (and only in the case of a forced choice experiment we may choose the parse with the highest probability from this distribution). When we estimate this probability distribution by statistical methods, we must establish the reliability of this estimate. This reliability is characterized by the probability of significant errors in the estimates of the probabilities of the various parses.

If a parse has probability p_i, and we try to estimate the probability of this parse by its frequency in a sequence of N independent samples, the variance in the estimated probability is $p_i(1 - p_i)/N$. Since $0 < p_i \leq 1$, the variance is always smaller than or equal to $1/(4N)$. Thus, the standard error σ, which is the square root of the variance, is always smaller than or equal to $1/(2\sqrt{N})$. This allows us to calculate a lower bound for N given an upper bound for σ, by $N \geq 1/(4\sigma^2)$. For instance, we obtain a standard error $\sigma \leq 0.05$ if $N \geq 100$.

We thus arrive at the following algorithm:

Algorithm 2: Estimating the parse probabilities in $O(\sigma^{-2})$ time
Given a derivation forest of a sentence and a threshold σ_M for the standard error:

$N :=$ the smallest integer larger than $1/(4\sigma_M{}^2)$
repeat N times:
    sample a random derivation from the derivation forest;
    store the parse generated by this derivation;
for each parse i:
    estimate the probability given the sentence by $p_i := \#(i) / N$

In the case of a forced choice experiment we select the parse with the highest probability from this distribution. Rajman (1995a) gives a correctness proof for Monte Carlo disambiguation; he shows that the probability of sampling a parse i from a derivation forest of a sentence w is equal to the conditional probability of i given w: $P(i \mid w)$.

The practical applicability of the above algorithm crucially depends on the choice for σ. If the probability of the most likely parse is very small, we must take σ also very small, which means that N gets very large (N grows inversely quadratic with σ). But since we actually estimate the conditional parse probabilities and not the absolute probabilities, it turns out that a σ of 0.05, or equivalently an N of 100, gives good convergence with satisfying results for the ATIS corpus (see next section). Whether small values for N may also work for other domains depends on the *skewness* of the conditional parse probability distribution (cf. Zipf 1935; Balcazar et al. 1988).

In the past few years, several further optimizations have been proposed for the disambiguation phase. For instance, Bod (1993b, 1995a) proposes to use only a small random subset of the corpus subtrees (5%) so as to reduce the search space. Goodman (1996) gives a polynomial time disambiguation strategy which disambiguates by means of the "maximum constituent parse" of a sentence (i.e. the parse which maximizes the expected number of correct constituents) rather than by the most probable parse. However, Goodman also shows that the "maximum constituent parse" may return parse trees that cannot be produced by the subtrees of DOP1 (Goodman 1996: 147). Goodman's claim that he found an efficient algorithm for DOP1 does therefore not hold, although his method may be used to compute a derivation forest for a sentence -- see §1 (for a general reply to Goodman 1996, see Bod 1996a). Sekine and Grishman (1995) propose to use only subtrees rooted with S or NP categories. But their method suffers considerably from undergeneration. Sima'an (1995, 1996a) gives a polynomial time strategy which starts out by using only the CFG-backbone of an STSG, after which the constraints imposed by the STSG are employed to further restrict the parse space and to select the "best" analysis. So far, Sima'an has used this method only for computing the most probable derivation of a sentence.

2.3 Cognitive aspects of Monte Carlo disambiguation

It is unlikely that people disambiguate sentences by sampling derivations, keeping track of the error probability of the most frequently resulting parse. Nevertheless, we believe there are certain properties of Monte Carlo disambiguation that are of psychological interest. The following lists some of them.

1. Although conceptually Monte Carlo disambiguation uses the total space of possible analyses, it tends to sample only the most likely ones. Very unlikely analyses may only be sampled after considerable time, and it is not guaranteed that *all* analyses are found in finite time. This matches with experiments on human sentence perception where implausible analyses are only perceived with great difficulty after considerable time; and often implausible analyses are not perceived at all (cf. Tanenhaus & Trueswell 1995).

2. Monte Carlo disambiguation does not necessarily give the same results for different sequences of samples, especially if different analyses in the top of the sampling distribution are almost equally likely. In the case there is more than one most probable analysis, Monte Carlo does not converge to one analysis but keeps alternating, however large the number of samples is made. In experiments with human sentence perception, it has often been shown that different analyses can be perceived for one sentence (e.g. MacDonald et al. 1994). And in case these analyses are equally plausible, e.g. due to a lack of disambiguation information, people may exhibit so-called fluctuation effects.

3. Monte Carlo disambiguation can be made parallel in a very straightforward way: N samples can be computed by N processing units, where equal outputs are reinforced. The more processing units are employed, the better the estimation. However, since the number of processing units is finite, there is never absolute confidence. In the field of neurobiology and cognitive science, the parallel nature of human information processing is widely recognized.

Despite these psychologically interesting properties, Monte Carlo algorithms could still be refined and extended if we want to create an optimal fit with the way humans process utterances. For instance, our algorithms are not fully incremental and recency is not (yet) brought into the picture (see chapter 8). However, in our experimental evaluation of DOP1 we will first of all be interested in comparing the most likely analysis of a sentence, as predicted by our Monte Carlo algorithms on the basis of a forced choice experiment, with the appropriate analysis of this sentence, as assigned by a native speaker.

5

Testing the model: can we restrict the productive units?

In this chapter, we establish some experimental properties of DOP1 on the basis of an English corpus of 750 sentence-analyses. The main goal of this chapter is to test the working hypothesis introduced in chapter 1: we test whether all (arbitrarily large and complex) previously seen fragments are in fact relevant for accurately predicting the appropriate analyses of new utterances. Our main question is therefore: can we restrict the fragments on linguistic or statistical grounds without diminishing the accuracy of predicting the appropriate representation? We will investigate restrictions in terms of overlap, size, lexicalization, frequency, and head vs. non-head words. We will also discuss the results of others who have tested our working hypothesis.

1 The test environment

Our experiments with DOP1 were carried out with a set of 750 sentence-analyses from the Air Travel Information System (ATIS) corpus (Hemphill et al. 1990), that were originally annotated in the Penn Treebank (Marcus et al. 1993). We corrected the mistagged words by hand and removed all epsilon productions and all analyses with so-called "pseudo-attachments". (In the last section of this chapter we will also report on experiments that were carried out with uncorrected ATIS annotations.) The ATIS corpus cannot stand as a collection of general natural language experiences. But if we assume that a corpus of general language experiences is divided into topic-dependent subcorpora (as we will argue in chapter 9), then the ATIS may stand as the subcorpus related to air travel information expressions. The following figure shows a typical ATIS tree (see Santorini 1990, 1991 for the annotation guidelines of the Penn Treebank).

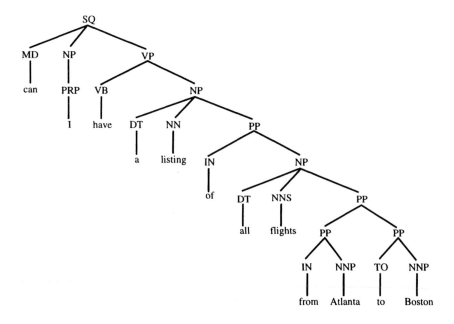

Figure 5.1. Example tree from the ATIS corpus

We use the blind testing method, as described in chapter 1, dividing the 750 ATIS trees into a 90% training set of 675 trees and a 10% test set of 75 trees. The division was random except for one constraint: that all words in the test set actually occurred in the training set (in the next chapter we extend DOP1 to cope with unknown words). The 675 training set trees were converted into fragments (i.e. subtrees) and were enriched with their corpus probabilities. The 75 sentences from the test set served as input sentences that were parsed with the fragments from the training set using a bottom-up chart parser and disambiguated by the Monte Carlo algorithms described in chapter 4. The most probable parses were estimated from probability distributions of 100 sampled derivations. As motivated in chapter 1, we use the notion of *parse accuracy* as our accuracy metric, defined as the percentage of test sentences for which the most probable parse is identical to the test set parse.

2 The base line

In our first experiment with DOP1, we did not apply any restrictions on the fragment collection. The parse accuracy obtained with the unrestricted fragment collection was 85%. We will use this number, together with the training/test set split, as the base line for studying the impact of the various fragment restrictions.

Ideally, we should study the impact of each fragment restriction on more than one training/test set split. However, the calculation of only one random derivation takes already about 6 seconds (on an SGI *Indigo* 2), and a full run on the 75 test set sentences, using 100 sampled derivations per sentence, takes more than 18 hours. We will therefore only check whether our base line result is not due to some unlikely random split. (Remember that all experimentally derived properties will also be tested on another corpus for another language in chapter 9.) On 10 random training/test set splits of the ATIS corpus we achieved an average parse accuracy of 84.2% with a standard deviation of 2.9%. Our 85% base line accuracy lies thus within the range of the standard deviation for 10 random training/test set splits.

3 The impact of overlapping fragments

DOP1 chooses as the most appropriate analysis of a sentence the most probable parse of that sentence, rather than the parse generated by the most probable derivation. The main difference between the most probable parse and the most probable derivation is that by summing up over probabilities of several derivations, the most probable parse takes into account *overlapping* fragments, while the most probable derivation does not.

Since the most probable derivation can be computed more efficiently (by Viterbi -- see chapter 4) than the most probable parse, it is worth checking whether there is a difference between the predictions of these two methods.

We thus calculated the accuracies based on the analyses generated by the most probable derivations of the test sentences. The parse accuracy obtained by the trees generated by the most probable derivations was 69%, which is much lower than the 85% base line parse accuracy obtained by the most probable parse. We conclude that overlapping fragments play an important role in predicting the appropriate representation of a sentence, and should not be deleted from the chart by Viterbi.

4 The impact of fragment size

Next, we tested the impact of the size of fragments on the parse accuracy. We already argued that large fragments can capture more lexical/syntactic dependencies than small ones. We are now interested in how much these dependencies actually lead to better predictions of the appropriate parse. Therefore we performed experiments with versions of DOP1 where the fragment collection is restricted to subtrees with a certain maximum depth (where the depth of a tree is defined as the length of the longest path from the root node to a frontier node). For instance, restricting the maximum depth of the subtrees to 1 gives us fragments that cover exactly one level of constituent structure, which makes DOP1 equivalent to a stochastic context-free grammar. For a maximum subtree-depth of 2, we obtain fragments that also cover two levels of constituent structure, which capture some more lexical/syntactic dependencies, etc. The following table shows the results of these experiments, where the parse accuracy for each maximal depth is given for both the most probable parse and for the parse generated by the most probable derivation (the accuracies are rounded off to the nearest integer).

depth of corpus-subtrees	parse accuracy	
	most probable parse	most probable derivation
1	47%	47%
≤2	68%	56%
≤3	79%	64%
≤4	83%	67%
≤5	84%	67%
≤6	84%	69%
unbounded	85%	69%

Table 5.1. Accuracy increases if larger corpus fragments are used

The table shows an increase in parse accuracy, for both the most probable parse and the most probable derivation, when enlarging the maximum depth of the subtrees. The table confirms that the most probable parse yields better accuracy than the most probable derivation, except for depth 1 where DOP1 is equivalent to SCFG (and where every parse is generated by exactly one derivation). The highest parse accuracy reaches 85%. Thus, at least within this tiny language domain, the hypothesis that larger productive units lead to better predictions of the appropriate sentence parse, is confirmed.

5 The impact of fragment lexicalization

In this section we test the impact of lexicalized fragments on the parse accuracy. By a lexicalized fragment we mean a fragment whose frontier contains one or more words. It may be obvious that the more words a fragment contains, the more lexical (collocational) dependencies are taken into account. To test the impact of lexical context on the parse accuracy, we performed experiments with different versions of DOP1 where the fragment collection is restricted to subtrees whose frontiers contain a certain maximum number of words; the maximal subtree depth was kept constant at 6.

These experiments are particularly interesting since we can simulate lexicalized grammars in this way. Lexicalized grammars have become increasingly popular in computational linguistics (e.g. Schabes 1992; Joshi & Srinivas 1994; Collins 1996, 1997; Charniak 1997a/b; Carroll & Weir 1997). However, all lexicalized grammars that we know of restrict the lexical context that is taken into account. It is a significant feature of the DOP approach that we can straightforwardly test the impact of the size of the lexical context.

The following table shows the results of our experiments, where the parse accuracy is given for both the most probable parse and the most probable derivation.

number of words in frontiers	parse accuracy	
	most probable parse	most probable derivation
≤1	75%	63%
≤2	80%	65%
≤3	83%	69%
≤4	83%	72%
≤6	83%	72%
≤8	87%	72%
unbounded	84%	69%

Table 5.2. Accuracy increases if more words are in fragment frontiers
(subtree-depth ≤ 6)

The table shows an initial increase in parse accuracy, for both the most probable parse and the most probable derivation, when enlarging the lexical context. For the most probable parse, the accuracy is stationary when the lexical context is enlarged from 4 to 6 words, but it increases again if the lexical context is enlarged to 8 words. For the most probable derivation, the parse accuracy reaches its maximum already at a lexicalization of 4 words. Note that the parse accuracy deteriorates if the lexicalization exceeds 8 words. Thus, there seems to be an optimal lexical context size for the ATIS corpus. The table confirms that the most probable parse yields better accuracy than the most probable derivation, also for different lexicalization sizes. In the following, we will therefore evaluate our results with respect to the most probable parse only.

If we compare table 5.1 with table 5.2, we observe that fragment size has a greater impact on the parse accuracy than fragment lexicalization: the accuracy grows considerably faster when depth is enlarged than when the number of words is enlarged. This goes against common wisdom that for language disambiguation lexical context is more important than syntactic context.

Instead of studying the importance of lexicalized fragments, we can also study the effect of *un*lexicalized fragments on the parse accuracy. In our previous experiments, we have retained all unlexicalized fragments. We performed an additional set of experiments where *unlexicalized* subtrees of a certain minimal depth are deleted from the fragment collection, while all *lexicalized* subtrees (up to depth 6) are retained. The following table shows the results of these experiments (for the most probable parse).

depth of eliminated unlexicalized subtrees	parse accuracy
≥1	79%
≥2	83%
≥3	83%
≥4	84%
≥5	84%
≥6	84%

Table 5.3. Accuracy increases if unlexicalized subtrees are retained

The table shows that accuracy increases if unlexicalized subtrees are retained, but that the accuracy is stationary after depth 4. For the ATIS we can thus safely discard unlexicalized fragments larger than depth 4.

6 The impact of fragment frequency

We may expect that highly frequent fragments contribute to a larger extent to the prediction of the appropriate parse than very infrequent fragments. While small fragments can occur very often, most larger fragments typically occur once. Nevertheless, large fragments contain much lexical/structural context, and can parse a large piece of an input sentence at once. Thus, it is interesting to see what happens if we systematically remove low-frequency fragments. We performed an additional set of experiments by restricting the fragment collection to subtrees with a certain minimum number of occurrences, but without applying any other restrictions.

frequency of subtrees	parse accuracy
≥1	85%
≥2	77%
≥3	45%
≥4	28%
≥5	16%
≥6	11%

Table 5.4. Accuracy decreases if lower bound on fragment frequency increases (for the most probable parse)

The above results indicate that low frequency fragments contribute significantly to the prediction of the appropriate analysis: the parse accuracy seriously deteriorates if low frequency fragments are discarded. This seems to contradict common wisdom that probabilities based on sparse data are not reliable. Since especially large fragments are once-occurring events, there seems to be a preference in DOP1 for an occurrence-based approach if enough context is provided: large fragments, even if they occur once, tend to contribute to the prediction of the appropriate parse, since they provide much contextual information. Although these fragments have very low probabilities, they tend to induce the most probable parse because fewer fragments are needed to construct a parse.

7 The impact of non-head words

In our previous experiments we have tested the working hypothesis by applying *quantitative* restrictions on the fragment collection (i.e. by restricting size, lexicalization, frequency). In this section we test the working hypothesis by applying a more *qualitative* restriction. It is rather uncontroversial that relations between head words are important for predicting the appropriate parse of a sentence (cf. Collins 1996; Charniak 1997a/b; Carroll & Weir 1997). Moreover, we have seen in chapter 3 (section 4) that relations between non-head words and head words can also contain important dependencies. But what about relations between non-head words only? In this section we study what happens if we delete fragments that only contain non-head words.

We start by defining a non-head word of a fragment. Given a fragment F with a root node category XP, by a non-head word of F we mean a frontier word of F that has a mother node category which is not of type X. For the special case of fragments rooted with a category of type S (e.g. SBAR, SBARQ, SINV, SQ) we define a non-head word as any frontier word with a mother node category which is not VB, VBG, etc. (i.e., not one of the ATIS "verb" categories).

For instance, the word *the* is a non-head word of the ATIS NP-fragment in figure 5.2, since the lexical category of *the* is not of type N (i.e., a noun).

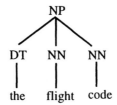

Figure 5.2. A subtree from the ATIS corpus

The other frontier words of this fragment (*flight* and *code*) are not non-head words since their mother node categories (NN in both cases) are of type N; i.e., in the Penn Treebank the part-of-speech tag NN stands for a noun singular. We thus note that a category of type X does not necessarily have a label *equal* to X. For instance, in the Penn Treebank the categories VB, VBD, VBG, VBN and VBP are all of type V (i.e., verb).

Our goal here is the deletion of lexicalized fragments that do not contain *any* word which could possibly be a head word. Thus the following fragment would be removed from the fragment collection, since the only word it contains is a non-head word:

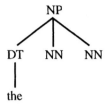

Figure 5.3. A subtree from the ATIS corpus with only a non-head word

We expect that the deletion of such a fragment will not harm the parse accuracy. Note that this fragment can, if needed, be generated by combining its two subfragments which are *not* removed by the non-head restriction.

The following fragment will be retained, since it does not contain only non-head words:

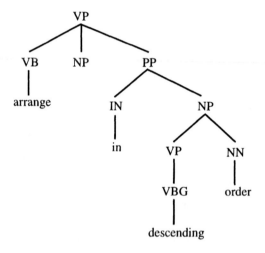

Figure 5.4. A subtree from the ATIS corpus with head words and non-head words

Such fragments guarantee that collocational dependencies between head and non-head words are retained. The fragment that results from taking out the verbs from figure 5.4, will be removed from the fragment collection:

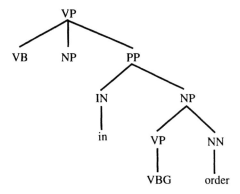

Figure 5.5. A subtree from the ATIS corpus with only non-head words

Whether the deletion of fragments like the one above harms the parse accuracy will be studied in the following experiments.

In our first experiment with the non-head restriction, we deleted all fragments whose frontier words were exclusively non-head words. We did not apply any other restrictions on the fragment collection. The parse accuracy obtained with this fragment collection was 74%, while with the complete fragment collection the parse accuracy was 85%. Evidently, fragments with only non-head words do contain important statistical dependencies that are not captured by other fragments. This goes against common wisdom that only head dependencies are important.

We then considered the number of non-head words in the fragment frontiers. We may expect that fragments that are lexicalized with only *one* non-head word (as in figure 5.3) are not important for the prediction of the appropriate parse. After eliminating these fragments from the fragment collection, but keeping all fragments with more than one non-head word, we obtained a parse accuracy of 80%, which is still worse than the original accuracy of 85%.

Again, this shows the difficulty of finding fragment elimination criteria that do not harm the accuracy: there is already an accuracy decrease if intuitively silly subtrees with just one non-head word are eliminated. However, the following example from the training set shows that such subtrees may not be silly at all, and can describe significant relations:

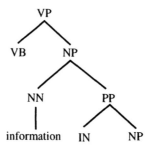

Figure 5.6. A relevant ATIS subtree with only one non-head word

This subtree covers many ATIS substrings that are of the form VB *information* IN ... (the tag IN stands for any preposition except *to*):

> *find information on* ...
> *get information from* ...
> *give information from/on* ...
> *have information on* ...
> *like information on* ...
> *list information about/on* ...
> *need information on* ...
> *see information from/in* ...
> *show information from/in/on* ...

In order to express the tendency that the above substrings occur with a specific structure, regardless the instantiations for VB and IN, we want to have a generalization over the verbs and prepositions but not over the noun *information*. The fragment in figure 5.6 exactly provides this generalization together with the preference for the specific structure. Moreover, the fragment also expresses that *information* tends to occur in the object position.

An even more interesting example is the subtree in figure 5.7, occurring in analyses for sentences such as *What are the nearby cities to the airport in Atlanta?* and *What are the nearby airports to Denver?*. The key-word in these sentences is the adjective *nearby*, which determines the correct attachment of the PPs *to the airport in Atlanta* and *to Denver*. This attachment is independent of the nominal heads *cities* and *airports* of which *nearby* is a modifier. Thus it is a non-head modifier which is essential for the prediction of the appropriate parse. A similar example would be the sentence *Show the nearest airport to Dallas*.

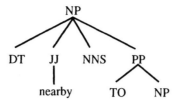

Figure 5.7. Another relevant ATIS subtree with only one non-head word

Clearly, such sentences are problematic for models that disambiguate on the basis of constituent heads only (e.g. Hindle & Rooth 1993; Collins 1996; Charniak 1997b), since these models would neglect the crucial non-head adjectives *nearby* and *nearest* as noted in chapter 3. The above examples may also be problematic for (stochastic) tree-adjoining grammar (Joshi et al. 1988; Resnik 1992), where an adjectival modifier such as *nearby* is treated as a separate auxiliary tree and thus the structure in figure 5.7 would not be allowed as one unit (cf. chapter 3, section 4.2). Even for (stochastic) Construction Grammar (Fillmore et al. 1988; Jurafsky 1996) this structure may be problematic since it does not reflect an idiomatic or semi-idiomatic meaning and might therefore not be included in the set of constructions.

We have thus seen that fragments with only one non-head word can describe linguistically and statistically interesting properties that contribute to the prediction of the appropriate parse.

Even words that are *always* non-head words in the ATIS corpus can express significant relations. The following fragment is only lexicalized with the word *the* which in the ATIS corpus always occurs as a non-head word. (The tag JJS refers to *superlative adjective* -- see Marcus et al. 1993.)

Figure 5.8. A relevant ATIS subtree with the non-head word *the*

This highly frequent ATIS fragment expresses the fact that English substrings of the pattern DT JJS NN are very likely to occur with the determiner *the* and are very unlikely to occur with other determiners. The following ATIS substrings are examples of this pattern (where some substrings also occur with a sister PP):

> *the cheapest fare*
> *the earliest flight*
> *the fewest number*
> *the highest range*
> *the latest flight*
> *the lowest cost*
> *the longest layover*
> *the shortest flight*

It should be noted that the deletion of these "exclusively non-head word subtrees" only slightly affects the prediction quality: the parse accuracy decreased with just one percent, i.e. with only one sentence-analysis.

Finally, we want to mention that if we remove all fragments with only head words, the parse accuracy was 70%. This is lower than the parse accuracy obtained by removing fragments with only non-head words (74%). Even if this difference is small, it suggests that, not very surprisingly, fragments with head words have a greater impact on the parse accuracy than fragments with non-head words.

8 Overview of the derived properties and discussion

We have thus observed the following properties for DOP1:

Overlap Property:
 The parse accuracy decreases if overlapping fragments are discarded.
Size Property:
 The parse accuracy increases if the size of the fragments increases.
Lexicalization Property:
 Maximal parse accuracy was achieved with fragments with up to 8 lexical items. Unlexicalized subtrees with depth > 4 may be discarded.

Size vs. Lexicalization Property:
Fragment size has a greater impact on the parse accuracy than fragment lexicalization.

Frequency Property:
The parse accuracy decreases if low-frequency fragments are discarded.

Non-head Property:
The parse accuracy decreases if fragments with non-head words are discarded.

Head Property:
The parse accuracy decreases if fragments with head words are discarded.

Head vs. Non-head Property:
Fragments with head words have a greater impact on the parse accuracy than fragments with non-head words.

These properties indicate that virtually all fragment elimination criteria diminish the prediction quality. We must keep in mind, however, that we have shown the validity of these properties only for one, rather impoverished, theory of representation (phrase structure trees), for one language (English) and for one tiny domain (ATIS). Nevertheless, our findings suggest that the productive units of natural language cannot be defined by a minimal set of non-redundant rules, but need to be defined by a large set of redundant structures with virtually no restriction on their form, size, lexicalization and (non-)head words.

In Bod (1996b), it is shown that the above properties (and thus our working hypothesis) also hold for the uncorrected ATIS corpus, although the base line parse accuracy is lower (68%). In chapter 9, we will test the above properties on an entirely different corpus for Dutch. In the past few years, several other researchers have tested our working hypothesis, sometimes by using different fragment elimination criteria and different evaluation strategies. We shortly go into their results.

Sima'an (1995, 1996a) reports on a number of experiments with DOP1 on the uncorrected ATIS corpus which confirms the increase in parse accuracy if larger corpus subtrees are taken into account. His experiments also show that the parse accuracy does not deteriorate if the number of nonterminals in the subtree frontiers is restricted to 2 (for the most probable derivation). Sima'an (1997a) also explores other fragment elimination criteria, which are based on Explanation-Based Learning (van Harmelen & Bundy 1988). Although these elimination criteria significantly speed up processing time, they diminish the parse accuracy.

Van der Hoeven (1995) tests DOP1 on a German annotated corpus of Railway Information expressions. His experiments support the hypothesis that the use of larger and more complex corpus fragments improves the prediction quality.

Sekine & Grishman (1995) give a version of DOP1 which constrains the corpus fragments to subtrees rooted with S and NP, and test their model on word strings from the Penn Treebank Wall Street Journal corpus (Marcus et al. 1993). In a personal communication, Sekine reports that the disambiguation accuracy increases if more complex corpus subtrees are taken into account.

Schütz (1996) applies DOP1 to the problem of part-of-speech tagging. Her experiments with a manually analyzed corpus of Dutch newspaper text (NRC Handelsblad) indicate that the tagging accuracy improves if the depth and lexicalization of the corpus subtrees is enlarged. She compares her results with a stochastic part-of-speech tagger based on a hidden markov model, and concludes that DOP's blending of lexical and syntactic information leads to better tagging accuracy than the use of lexical information alone.

Bonnema (1996) confirms our working hypothesis for a version of the ATIS corpus in which the syntactic nodes are manually enriched with logical-semantic representations. Bonnema also shows that the use of semantic annotations leads to higher syntactic parse accuracy than the use of syntactic annotations alone.

Goodman (1996) gives a version of DOP1 which disambiguates by means of the so-called "maximum constituent parse". As noted in chapter 4, Goodman shows that the maximum constituent parse may return parse trees that cannot be produced by the subtrees of DOP1 (Goodman 1996: 147). In his PhD thesis, however, Goodman also computes the most probable parse by Monte Carlo sampling, reporting that its performance is almost identical to the maximum constituent parse (Goodman 1998). Although Goodman does not evaluate the parse accuracy for different subtree sizes, he compares his results to a replication of Pereira & Schabes (1992) on the same data. On the corrected ATIS corpus, the Pereira & Schabes method achieves an average "zero-crossing brackets accuracy" of 79.2% while DOP1 obtains 86.1% (Goodman 1998: 179). Goodman shows that this accuracy-increase of 6.9%, or error-reduction of 33%, is statistically significant. On a minimally edited version of the ATIS corpus, DOP1 also outperforms Pereira & Schabes (65.9% vs. 63.9%), but the differences are not statistically significant. Goodman (1998) also criticizes some of my previous results with part-of-speech strings from the corrected ATIS corpus (Bod 1995b). He gives an analysis showing that there is maximally a 15.7% chance of getting a test set with my reported 96% parse accuracy (Goodman 1998: 183). While I agree with Goodman's criticism that experimental results should be averaged on several different test corpora (as I did for the base line accuracy in this chapter), I want to stress that what I have been interested in is not whether DOP1 obtains x% or y% accuracy -- this differs from corpus to corpus -- but whether DOP1 displays an increase in parse accuracy if larger and more complex subtrees are used.

Zavrel (1996) compares DOP1 with a disambiguation technique which is based on Memory Based Learning (Aha et al. 1991). Although Zavrel does not evaluate the parse accuracy for different subtree sizes, he shows by paired t-tests that the DOP approach significantly outperforms the Memory Based Learning approach.

In van Zaanen (1997), DOP1 is extended to the problem of error correction. His experiments with four different extensions of DOP1 confirm that the (correction) accuracy improves if larger context is used.

Charniak (1996, 1997a) gives a version of DOP1 in which the subtrees are limited to depth 1. As we have noted, such a model is equivalent to a stochastic context-free grammar (SCFG). However, Charniak's model is different from previous SCFGs (e.g. Fujisaki et al. 1989; Jelinek et al. 1990; Schabes et al. 1993) in that his model, like DOP1, uses *all* (depth-1) corpus subtrees regardless their frequency or redundancy, and estimates their probabilities directly by their relative frequencies. Charniak performs experiments with part-of-speech strings from the Wall Street Journal corpus, reporting that his system "outperforms all other non-word-based statistical parsers/grammars on this corpus" (Charniak 1996: 1031). Thus, even if Charniak's approach constitutes a less-than-optimal version of DOP1, it shows that DOP's direct estimation of rules and probabilities works better than re-estimation techniques based on Inside-Outside training (Pereira & Schabes 1992; Schabes et al. 1993) or Transformation-Based Learning (Brill 1993).

Carroll & Weir (1997) compare DOP1 with a number of alternative probabilistic frameworks: SCFG (Booth & Thompson 1973), SLTAG (Schabes 1992; Resnik 1992) and Link Grammar (Lafferty et al.

1992). They evaluate the adequacy of each framework with respect to the structural units that can be statistically differentiated (not to be confused with the "stochastic generative capacity" of a framework -- see chapter 3), and show that there is a subsumption lattice where SCFG is at the bottom and DOP1 at the top. That is, DOP1 is able to differentiate probabilistically all structural units that the other frameworks can, while DOP1 is the only framework which can statistically relate constituents that are arbitrarily widely separated -- structurally as well as sequentially. Carroll & Weir illustrate this by the sentence *The emaciated man starved*, first published in Bod (1995b), where there is an interdependency between the NP-modifier *emaciated* and the VP-head *starved*, which can moreover be arbitrarily widely separated (e.g. in *The emaciated man I saw yesterday starved*).

Coleman & Pierrehumbert (1997) develop a DOP model based on a corpus of phonotactically annotated words. Although their model allows for (phonotactic) subtrees of arbitrary depth, they do not evaluate the parse accuracy for different depths. Instead, Coleman & Pierrehumbert evaluate the predictions of their model against experimentally obtained judgments of the phonotactic acceptability of nonsense words. They show that by using the frequencies of all subparts of annotated words, their model accounts for the fact that well-formed subparts of an otherwise ill-formed word can alleviate the ill-formed parts, especially if their frequency is high. Coleman & Pierrehumbert argue that this finding is contrary to the predictions of Optimality Theory (Prince & Smolensky 1993), as this approach does not recognize a mechanism by which the well-formedness of lexically attested parts ameliorates the unacceptability of the unattested parts. In DOP, on the other hand, the accumulation of (frequencies of) well-formed parts can overrule the unacceptability of low-frequency parts.

We thus note that there is a large and rapidly growing class of computational models that use the Data-Oriented Parsing approach. Independent experiments with different versions of this approach indicate that it outperforms other (probabilistic) methods. Although these results are encouraging, we again want to stress that what matters is not whether DOP obtains x% or y% accuracy -- this differs from corpus to corpus and depends on its domain and size -- but that DOP displays an increase in prediction quality if larger and more complex fragments are taken into account -- and that this holds for all corpora.

6

Learning new words

In the previous chapter, we derived a number of properties of DOP1 which supports the hypothesis that language processing works with a large set of redundant structures rather than with a minimal set of non-redundant rules. Our experiments were, however, based on test sentences whose words are known in the training set. In fact, DOP1 cannot parse or disambiguate sentences with unknown words, as it only uses fragments that are literally found in the training set. In this chapter, we start with an investigation of what is involved in extending DOP1 to cope with unknown words.

Although well-recognized in natural language processing, the problem of unknown words is ignored in linguistic theory. Modern linguistic theories view languages as infinite sets of sentences, defined by *finite* sets of elements (rules and lexical items). The problem of unknown words is thus non-existent from such a point of view. However, language users *do* process sentences with previously unseen words and they have expectations about the structure and meaning that can be assigned to such sentences. Moreover, in first language acquisition a language learner is almost continuously confronted with new words -- and with new syntactic structures. But while the total set of possible syntactic structures may be assumed to be universal or innate, such an assumption cannot be sustained for lexical items. We therefore need a theory that deals with unknown words and the expectations language users have when confronted with previously unseen words.

1 The model DOP2

As a first tentative solution to unknown words we propose the model DOP2. DOP2 is a very simple extension of DOP1: assign all lexical categories to each unknown word, and select the most probable parse among the parses of the resulting "sentences" by means of DOP1. Thus, unknown words are assigned a lexical category such that their surrounding or partial parse has maximum probability. We shall refer to this method as the *partial parse method* (we use the word *partial* in the sense that it is not the full sentence-parse which is assigned a probability, but only a *partial* parse without the unknown words).

The partial parse method has been used in previous systems that deal with unknown words. A very similar method was applied as early as 1979 in a deterministic parsing system by Carbonell (1979), who called it the *project and integrate* method. With the renewed interest in stochastic grammars, several stochastic parsers have adopted the partial parse method in order to obtain some robustness in dealing with unexpected input.

For its simplicity, the partial parse method may seem attractive. However, it is not founded on a sound statistical basis. For instance, the method does not provide probabilities for the parses of the whole sentence, but only for the parses of the "sentence" without the unknown words. Formally, the probability of a parse that contains at least one unknown word is equal to zero in DOP2. It is nevertheless interesting to study where and why the partial parse method can solve unknown words and where and why it cannot. We will see that the outcome of this study leads to a better insight of the properties of unknown words and triggers the development of a better model.

Remember that according to the DOP paradigm, once a sentence with an unknown word is analyzed, it is added to the corpus and the unknown word is learned. But it may be forgotten again if it is never re-invoked, depending on the nature of the recency function -- see chapter 8.

One may raise the question as to whether it makes sense to learn unknown words only on the basis of their lexical/syntactic context. Simple morphological structure, such as word endings, often give reliable clues for the lexical categories of new words. But if we want to account for unknown words whose morphology does not convey any clue for their category, we need a theory that predicts the best category solely on the basis of context (in the absence of semantic or pragmatic information).

2   Experiments with DOP2

To test the adequacy of DOP2 with respect to unknown words, we employ the same parsing and disambiguation algorithms as developed for DOP1 (chapter 4). The only difference is that we need to establish the unknown words of an input sentence beforehand and label them with all lexical categories. As to the test environment, we now randomly split the ATIS into a training/test set *without* the constraint that test set words occur in the training set. As before, we use the notion of parse accuracy to indicate the percentage of the test sentences for which the most likely parse is identical to the parse in the test set.

The 75 test sentences contained 33 words that were unknown in the training set. This corresponded to 26 test sentences with one or more unknown words and 49 sentences with only known words. In order to study the effect of fragment size on the parse accuracy, we performed similar experiments as in the previous chapter, constraining the maximum depths of the training set fragments. The following table gives the results of these experiments up to fragment depth 3. (We used no fragments larger than depth 3, since our method of assigning *all* lexical categories to unknown words leads to extremely large derivation forests -- see also chapter 7.)

depth of corpus-subtrees	parse accuracy sentences with unknown words	parse accuracy sentences with only known words	parse accuracy for all sentences
1	15%	39%	31%
≤2	35%	69%	57%
≤3	42%	73%	63%

Table 6.1. Parse accuracy obtained with DOP2 for the ATIS corpus

We notice that the parse accuracy improves if the maximum depth of the fragments increases (as in chapter 5). However, it is disappointing that *only* 42% of the sentences with unknown words are parsed correctly. On the other hand, if plain DOP1 were used, the accuracy would have been 0% for these sentences.

If we look at the sentences with only known words, we see that the maximum parse accuracy of 73% is considerably higher than for sentences with unknown words, and it is comparable with the 79% parse accuracy of DOP1 in the previous chapter (for the same fragment depth).

3 Evaluation: what goes wrong?

The experimental results suggest the need for a careful evaluation. We will evaluate the results for subtree-depth ≤ 3, since it is here that highest accuracy is achieved in our experiments. To start with the good news, we show some sentences with unknown words that were correctly parsed and disambiguated by DOP2 (the unknown words are printed bold).

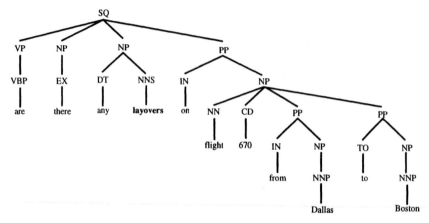

Figure 6.1. Parse for *Are there any **layovers** on flight 670 from Dallas to Boston?*

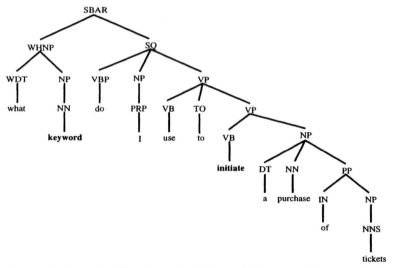

Figure 6.2. Parse for *What **keyword** do I use to **initiate** a purchase of tickets?*

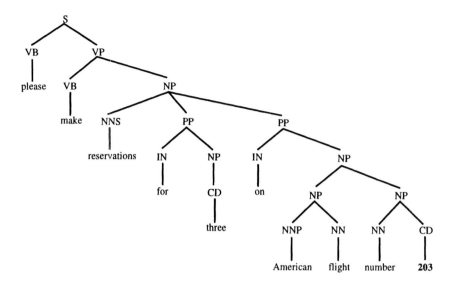

Figure 6.3. Parse for *Please make reservations for three on American flight number 203*

These parses show that the lexico-syntactic context of unknown words can correctly predict their lexical categories together with the appropriate parses.

Let us now consider the bad news, and look at some sentences with unknown words for which the most likely parse did not match the test set parse. The unknown words are again given in bold.

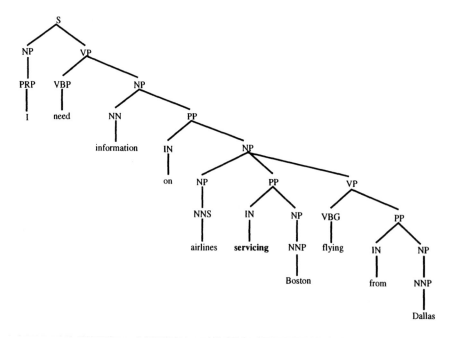

Figure 6.4. Incorrect most likely parse for the sentence *I need information on airlines **servicing** Boston flying from Dallas.*

In this parse the unknown word *servicing* is incorrectly tagged as a preposition (IN), and consequently attached to a prepositional phrase (PP). This may be explained by the very frequent occurrences in the ATIS corpus of prepositional phrases of the form in figure 6.5:

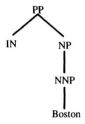

Figure 6.5. PP subtree in the ATIS corpus

What happened, is, that *airlines servicing Boston* was interpreted as something like *airlines from Boston*. It would be interesting if the incorrect tagging of *servicing* could be interpreted as the preposition *to*, which is distributionally and semantically very similar to *servicing*. Unfortunately this is not possible, since the Penn Treebank provides the tag TO for the preposition *to*, and the tag IN for all other prepositions. However, the assignment of a PP to the constituent *servicing Boston* is semantically correct. The only reason for *not* annotating *servicing Boston* as a PP, is the connection of *servicing* with the verb *service*; but in order to recognize this in the parsing process we would also need morphological annotations. In the ATIS corpus, *servicing* is tagged as a VBG (verb gerund) and is attached to a VP:

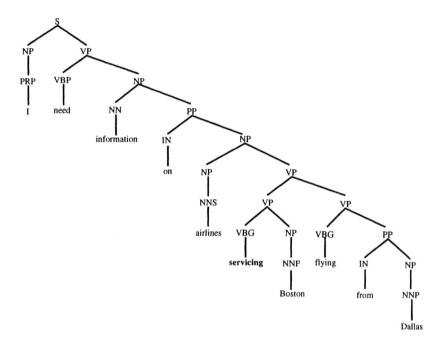

Figure 6.6. ATIS parse for the sentence *I need information on airlines servicing Boston flying from Dallas.*

Another test sentence whose parse did not match the test set parse is the following:

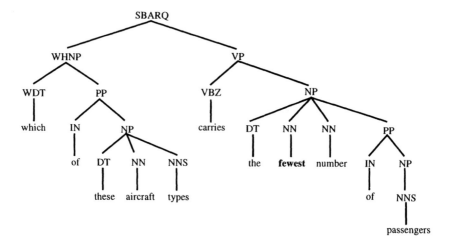

Figure 6.7. Incorrect most likely parse for *Which of these aircraft types carries the fewest number of passengers?*

In this parse, the unknown word *fewest* is incorrectly tagged as an NN (noun singular), while its correct part of speech tag according to the ATIS is JJS (superlative adjective). This is because NPs like figure 6.8(a) are more frequent in the ATIS than NPs like figure 6.8(b) (mainly due to the highly frequent NP *the flight number of ...*) . Thus in the absence of a dictionary and morphological annotations, *fewest* is interpreted as a noun in this domain.

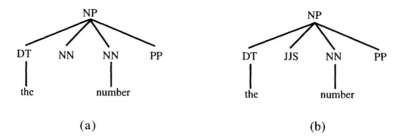

(a)   (b)

Figure 6.8. Two NP subtrees

The above examples show that the analysis of unknown words by simply maximizing the probability of their lexico-syntactic context can give biased predictions. The question is whether these biased predictions inherently depend on the meta-principle of letting the statistics decide or whether they are the consequence of the partial parse method which does not allow for computing the probability of the *full* sentence parse.

The following incorrectly parsed test sentence gives an indication of the nature of the biases that in fact occur with the partial parse method.

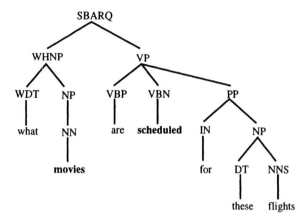

Figure 6.9. Incorrect parse for *What **movies** are **scheduled** for these flights?*

The only error in this parse is the part-of-speech assignment for the unknown word *movies*. This word is tagged as an NN (noun singular), while it should have been tagged as an NNS (noun plural). The explanation for this could be that in WHNP subtrees the word *what* is more likely to be followed by a singular noun than by a plural noun. This tagging error leads, however, to a disagreement in number between the subject *movies*, tagged as a singular noun, and the verb *are*, tagged as a plural verb (VBP). This absence of number agreement is striking since there is in fact a large SBARQ subtree of depth 3 in the training set that *maintains* the number agreement (between a plural subject and the plural verb -- see figure 6.10). Given the preference in DOP for parses that can be constructed by largest possible fragments, one would expect the right tagging of *movies*. But instead of using this large SBARQ subtree, DOP2 used a smaller WHNP subtree for parsing the sentence. Evidently, the WHNP subtree occurs so much more frequently with respect to the

SBARQ subtree, that the most probable partial parse was generated if the WHNP subtree was used.

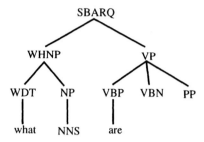

Figure 6.10. A large SBARQ-subtree from the training set maintaining number agreement

Something similar has happened in parsing the sentence *What are the amenities?*, where the unknown word *amenities* is incorrectly tagged as a singular noun leading once again to a number disagreement with the verb *are* (figure 6.11).

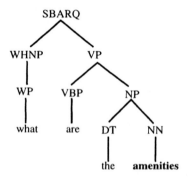

Figure 6.11. Incorrect parse for *What are the **amenities?***

Notice that DOP1 usually satisfies number agreement, not because it contains an explicit agreement mechanism, but because it prefers parses that can be constructed by larger subtrees. It seems now, that this property cannot be guaranteed by the abberated statistics emerging from DOP2.

4 The problem of unknown-category words

If we study the most probable parses for the test sentences *without* unknown words, we discover that for some of these sentences no parse could be generated, not because a word was unknown, but because an ambiguous word required a lexical category which it did not have in the training set. We will call these words *unknown-category words.*

To illustrate this, consider the following three test sentences with unknown-category words, of which the first two sentences could not be parsed at all, while the third was parsed inappropriately (the unknown-category words are printed bold):

***Return** to first inquiry.*

*Where is the **stop** for USAir flight number 37 from Philadelphia to San Francisco?*

*How much does flight number 83 **cost** one-way?*

In the first sentence, the word *return* is in the training set only known as a noun (NN), whereas its lexical category in this sentence is a verb (VB). In the second sentence, the word *stop* is only known as a verb (VB) in the training set, while its required category is NN. In the third sentence, the verb *cost* was only known as a noun in the training set, while it should have been a verb. Nevertheless, this last sentence could be parsed, though it led to the nonsensical most probable parse in figure 6.12.

Notice that richer, morphological annotations would not be of any help here: the words *return*, *stop* and *cost* do not have a morphological structure on the basis of which their possible lexical categories can be predicted.

These examples show that we are not only uncertain about the categories of unknown words but also about the categories of known words -- a problem which we completely neglected in the previous chapter. We might propose that *all words should be treated as unknown*, such that all words can in principle have any lexical category. However, it is easy to see that DOP2 would then give completely erroneous predictions: if all words are assigned all lexical categories, then every sentence of the same length will get the same most probable parse. And if we treat only the *open class* words as unknown, we will get this kind of bias for those parts of the sentences that consist of only open class words.

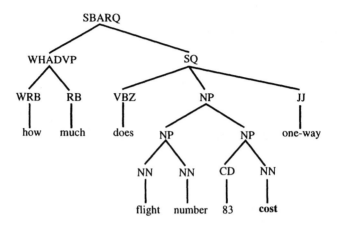

Figure 6.12. Incorrect parse for *How much does flight number 83 **cost** one-way?*

We want to stress that the problem of unseen and unknown-category words is *not* an artifact that is due to the tiny size of the ATIS corpus. No corpus of any size will ever contain all possible uses of all possible words. Adding a dictionary to the corpus does not solve the problem, because there will be domain-specific word senses, proper nouns, abbreviations etc. that do not occur in this dictionary. A statistically adequate treatment of unknown words and unknown-category words will always be needed. The use of the tiny ATIS should just be seen as illustrative for any larger corpus.

We may wonder whether it is possible to do better than the partial parse method. This will be the topic of the next chapter.

7

Learning new structures

We have seen that the partial parse method, as employed by DOP2, yields poor predictions for the analyses of sentences with unknown words. For sentences with so-called unknown-category words, the method appeared to be completely erroneous. A reason for these shortcomings may be the statistical inadequacy of DOP2: it does not treat unseen and unknown-category words as (part of the) productive units, and thus these words are not integrated in the underlying stochastic process.

To account for the expectations people have about sentence-analyses that cannot be produced by *known* subtrees, a DOP model must predict the probabilities of *unknown* subtrees. We thus view a person's knowledge of a language not as complete, but as a sample of a larger population (to which a person's language knowledge converges). The problem is then to account for people's expectations of structures that are out of this sample and to assign probabilities to these structures. In the following, we will show how this problem can be solved with a minimum of statistical assumptions.

1 The problem of unknown structures

By an unknown structure we mean a subtree which does not occur in the training set, but which may show up in an additional set of trees (like the test set). We will restrict ourselves to subtrees whose unknownness depends only on unknown terminals, since we are concerned here with unknown(-category) words only. Thus, we assume that if there is an unknown subtree in the test set, then there is a subtree in the training set which differs from the unknown subtree only in some of its terminals. The assumption that only the terminals in unknown subtrees are unknown can as well be withdrawn, although this may lead to a space of possible subtrees which is currently computationally impractical.

Even with the current restriction, the problem is far from trivial. Two main questions are:

1. How can we derive unknown subtrees?

2. How can we estimate the probabilities of unknown subtrees?

As to the first question, we are not able to generate the space of unknown subtrees in advance, as we do not know the unknown terminals in advance. But given a certain input sentence, we can derive the unknown subtrees that are needed for analyzing this sentence by allowing the unknown words and unknown-category words of the sentence to *mismatch* with the lexical terminals of the training set subtrees -- provided that we know which are the unknown(-category) words, a problem to which we will come back later. The result of a mismatch between a subtree and one or more unknown(-category) words is a subtree in which the terminals are replaced by the words with which it mismatched. In other words, these subtree-terminals are treated as if they are wildcards. As a result, we may get subtrees in the derivation forest that do not occur in the training set.

The effect of the mismatch method is illustrated by the example in figure 7.1. In parsing the NP *the **aircraft** code*, the unknown word ***aircraft*** mismatches with the terminal *flight* which it replaces; the words *the* and *code* do not mismatch with subtree-terminals. (There can of course be other NP-subtrees that parse *the **aircraft** code* in this way.)

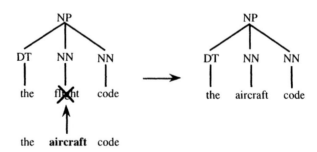

Figure 7.1. Illustration of the mismatch method for deriving unknown subtrees

The mismatch method has one bottleneck: it can only be used if we know which words of an input sentence are unknown or have an unknown category. It is easy to establish the *unknown* words of a sentence, but it is unclear how to establish the *unknown-category* words. Since every word is a potential unknown-category word (even closed-class words, if the corpus is small), we ideally need to treat all words of a sentence as possible unknown-category words. Thus, any subtree-terminal is in principle allowed to mismatch with any word of the input sentence; this means that any word can be "reanalyzed". (Of course, we may raise the question as to whether such a model is not *too* powerful. In section 5 of this chapter we will derive some properties of this DOP model, showing among other things that the most likely parse displays a preference for a *minimal* number of mismatches.)

How can we estimate the probability of a subtree that appears as a result of the mismatch method in the derivation forest, but not in the training set? Obviously, we must abandon the approach used in DOP1, where probabilities were simply identified with corpus occurrence frequencies. Instead, we will treat the space of subtrees as a sample of a larger population. As motivated in the beginning of this chapter, we believe that such an approach is also reasonable from a cognitive point of view.

An unknown subtree which has a zero probability in a sample may have a non-zero probability in the total population. Moreover, observed subtrees may also have population probabilities that differ from their relative corpus occurrence frequencies. The problem is how to estimate the population probability of a subtree on the basis of the observed corpus only. Much work in statistics is concerned with the fitting of particular distributions to sample data; to apply these methods we must know which of these distributions should be assumed. A method which is largely independent of the probability distribution in the population is the *Good-Turing* method (Good 1953). It only assumes that the sample is obtained at random from the total population. We will propose this method for estimating the population probabilities of subtrees. Good-Turing is often used in the field of speech recognition and part-of-speech tagging, but it is rather new in the field of syntactic parsing. We will therefore briefly describe the method in the following section (which heavily relies on Church & Gale 1991).

2 Good-Turing: estimating the population probabilities of (un)seen types

The Good-Turing method, suggested by A. M. Turing in a 1941 personal communication to I. J. Good (Good 1953), estimates the expected population probability of a type by adjusting its observed sample frequency. We will refer to r as the *observed* frequency of a type, and to $r*$ as the *adjusted* frequency of r. In order to estimate $r*$, Good-Turing uses an additional notion, represented by n_r, which is defined as the number of types which occur r times in an observed sample. Thus, n_r can be seen as the frequency of frequency r. The entire distribution $\{n_1, n_2, n_3, ...\}$ is available in addition to the different rs. The Good-Turing estimator uses this extra information for computing the adjusted frequency $r*$ as

$$r* = (r+1)\frac{n_{r+1}}{n_r}$$

The expected probability of a type t with observed frequency $\#(t) = r$ is estimated by $r*/N$, where N is the total number of observed types. Notice that the adjusted frequencies satisfy

$$\sum n_r\, r*\, /\, N = 1$$

Good-Turing obtains good estimates for $r*/N$ if n_r is large. We will see that for our applications, n_r tends to be large for small frequencies r, while on the other hand, if n_r is small, r is usually large and needs not to be adjusted.[7]

For the adjustment of the frequencies of *unseen* types, where $r = 0$, $r*$ is equal to n_1/n_0, where n_0 is the number of types that we have not seen. n_0 is equal to the difference between the total number of types and the number of observed types. Thus, in order to calculate the adjusted frequency of an unseen type, we need to know the total number of types in the population. Good (1953) shows that the proportion of the population represented by the sample is approximately equal to $1 - n_1/N$. Notice that

---

[7] This phenomenon is formalized by Zipf's Law, which states that frequency is roughly proportional to inverse rank (Zipf 1935).

the Good-Turing estimator does not differentiate among the types that have not been seen: the adjusted frequencies of all unseen types are identical.

For a more elaborate treatment of Good-Turing and some enhancements of it, we refer to Church & Gale (1991), Gale & Sampson (1995) and Samuelsson (1996). A very instructive paper on the method is Nadas (1985), who presents three different statistical ways to obtain Turing's formula.

3   Using Good-Turing to adjust the frequencies of subtrees

The use of the Good-Turing method in natural language technology is not new. It is commonly applied in speech recognition and part-of-speech tagging for adjusting the frequencies of (un)seen word sequences (e.g. Jelinek 1985; Katz 1987; Church & Gale 1991). In stochastic parsing, Good-Turing has to our knowledge never been used. Stochastic parsing systems either use a closed lexicon (e.g. Black, Garside & Leech 1993; Fujisaki et al. 1989), or use a two step approach where first the words are tagged by a stochastic tagger, after which the part-of-speech tags (with or without the words) are parsed by a stochastic parser. The latter approach has become increasingly popular (e.g. Pereira & Schabes 1992; Schabes et al. 1993; Weischedel et al. 1993; Briscoe 1994; Magerman 1995; Collins 1996, 1997). Notice, however, that the tagger used in this two step approach often uses Good-Turing to adjust the observed frequencies of n-grams. So why not apply Good-Turing directly to the rules of a stochastic grammar?

This lack of interest in applying Good-Turing to the structural units of a stochastic grammar may be due to the assumption that grammars need to be defined by *finite* sets of elements. The existence of unobserved rules is thus unacceptable from such a (competence) point of view.[8] But from a performance point of view, it is very well acceptable that not all productive units have been seen; therefore we will put forward the Good-Turing estimator as a cognitively adequate extension of DOP1.

How can Good-Turing be used for adjusting the frequencies of known and unknown subtrees? It may be evident that it is too rough to apply Good-Turing to all subtrees together. We must distinguish between subtrees of different root node categories, since in DOP, the collections

---

[8] Although the opposite opinion may be heard as well (e.g. Sampson 1987).

of subtrees of a particular root node category constitute different distributions, for each of which the probabilities sum up to one. Therefore, Good-Turing is applied to each subtree-class separately, that is, to the S-subtrees, NP-subtrees, VP-subtrees, N-subtrees, V-subtrees, etc. As in the previous chapter, we will use only the subtrees up to depth three.

In order to clarify this, we show in table 7.1 the adjusted frequencies for the class of the 118348 NP-subtrees from the ATIS training set. The first column of the table shows the observed frequencies of NP-subtrees from zero to six. The second column shows n_r, the number of NP-subtrees that had those frequencies in the training set (the estimation of n_0 is a special case and will be dealt with shortly). The third column shows the adjusted frequencies as calculated by the Good-Turing formula. For instance, for $r = 2$, $n_r = 9057$ and $n_{r+1} = 4161$, thus $r^* = (r+1)\, n_{r+1} / n_r = (2+1) \cdot 4161/9057 = 1.37$.

r	n_r	r^*
0	8300000000	0.0000073
1	60416	0.30
2	9057	1.37
3	4161	1.86
4	1944	1.99
5	773	3.74
6	482	4.37

Table 7.1. Adjusted frequencies for ATIS NP-subtrees

The calculations for $r = 0$ rest on an estimation of n_0, the number of NP-subtrees that have not been seen. n_0 is equal to the difference between the total number of distinct NP-subtrees and the number of distinct NP-subtrees seen. Thus, we must estimate the total number of possible NP-subtrees. This number may be computed by Good's approximation formula for the sample/population proportion $(1 - n_1/N)$; but a direct application of this formula would lead to severe underestimation of the number of possible NP-subtrees, since our method allows *any* subtree-terminal to mismatch with *any* word of an input sentence. We will therefore use Good's approximation formula only for estimating the total number of ATIS words, after which we derive the number of possible NP-subtrees by computing the number of different attachments of ATIS words to the part-of-speech tags of the unlexicalized NP-subtrees from the training set.

The estimation of (1) the ATIS vocabulary size, (2) the total number of distinct NP-subtrees, (3) the number of unseen NP-subtrees n_0, and (4) the adjusted frequency for unseen NP-subtrees, is accomplished as follows:

(1) There are 1351 word types in the ATIS training set, of which 307 occur once; thus the sample/population proportion is approximately equal to $1 - 307/1351 = 0.773$. This gives us a number of $1353 / 0.773 = 1750$ word types for the ATIS vocabulary size.

(2) The total number of NP-subtrees (that can be the result of the mismatch method) is calculated as the number of different attachments of 1750 dummies to the unlexicalized NP-subtrees from the training set. This yields a number of $8.29766 \cdot 10^9$ distinct subtrees. To this number, the number of distinct unlexicalized NP-subtrees must be added (12429), yielding $8.29767 \cdot 10^9$ types for the total number of distinct NP-subtrees.

(3) The number of unseen types n_0 is the difference between the total number of distinct NP-subtrees, $8.29767 \cdot 10^9$, and the observed number of distinct NP-subtrees, $\Sigma_{r>0} n_r = 77479$; that is $8.29767 \cdot 10^9 - 77479 = 8.29759 \cdot 10^9$. Notice that n_0 is approximately equivalent to the total number of NP-subtrees, which means that hardly any of the possible NP-subtrees (that can be the result of our permissive mismatch method) have been seen.

(4) Finally, the adjusted frequency for unseen NP-subtrees is calculated by Good-Turing as $n_1/n_0 = 60416 / 8.3 \cdot 10^9 = 0.0000073$. Thus, the Good-Turing method assigns a frequency to unseen NP-subtrees, as if we had seen each of them 0.0000073 times instead of zero times.[9]

---

[9] This extremely small frequency for unseen NP-subtrees is the consequence of treating *all* words as unknown-category words. If we restrict the class of possible unknown-category words, the number of unseen NP-subtrees gets smaller and their adjusted frequency consequently larger.

4 The model DOP3

DOP3 is very similar to DOP1. What is different in DOP3 is (1) a much larger space of subtrees, which is extended to include subtrees in which one or more terminals are substituted by input string words, and (2) the frequencies of the subtrees, that are now adjusted by the Good-Turing method. The probability definitions of a derivation, parse and string in DOP3 are the same as in DOP1. That is, the probability of a derivation is equal to the product of the probabilities of its subtrees, the probability of a parse tree is equal to the sum of the probabilities of its derivations, and the probability of a string is equal to the sum of the probabilities of its parses.

It might seem that DOP3 is, like DOP1, formally equivalent to Stochastic Tree-Substitution Grammar: the subtrees of DOP3 can be described by elementary trees of an STSG and the subtree probabilities of DOP3 correspond to the probabilities of the elementary trees of an STSG. However, in a grammar, all productive units (in our case subtrees) need to be defined beforehand. In DOP3, it is impossible to know all subtrees beforehand, since they are only derived during the parsing process by the mismatch method. We already noticed before that DOP models are in contrast with the linguistic notion of a grammar; we now notice that the model DOP3 cannot even be described anymore by the mathematical notion of a grammar. DOP3 is an adaptive dynamic system where the set of productive units changes as soon as new input comes in.

Although DOP3 is not equivalent to STSG, this is only due to the rigid definition of a grammar, where the set of productive units is assumed to be a priori known. In computational practice, we can very easily extend the parsing algorithms designed for STSG to DOP3, by allowing the terminals of subtrees to mismatch with the words of the input sentence. After assigning the adjusted probabilities to the subtrees in the resulting derivation forest, the most probable parse can be estimated by the Monte Carlo algorithms of chapter 4.

5 Cognitive aspects of DOP3

DOP3 posits that people have expectations about subtrees that never occurred before. In this section we derive some properties showing that DOP3 displays the desirable preferences for the most probable parses.

Preference for parses containing a minimal number of mismatches

The fact that DOP3 assigns very low frequencies to unknown subtrees (that consequently get even lower probabilities), implies that a most probable parse tends to contain a minimal number of unknown subtrees. Thus, if a parse can be generated by few (or zero) unknown subtrees, it tends to get a higher probability than a parse which is generated by using many unknown subtrees. This means that there is a preference for parses constructed by a minimal number of mismatches between subtree-terminals and input words. In other words: DOP3 tends to generalize over a minimal number of words.

As an example, consider the ATIS test sentence *Return to first inquiry*. In chapter 6 (section 4), we have seen that this sentence could not be parsed by DOP2 due to the unknown-category word *return* which in the training set only occurs as a noun. In DOP3, this sentence can be parsed if *return* mismatches with a subtree-terminal tagged as a verb. However, this sentence can also be parsed if *first* mismatches with a noun (such that *Return to first* is analyzed as an NP) and *inquiry* mismatches with a verb. The latter relabeling would yield a parse which can be generated by derivations containing more unknown subtrees than the first relabeling. This parse would therefore get a lower probability.

Preference for mismatches with open-class words

Another property of DOP3 is that *parses that generalize over open-class words are preferred to parses that generalize over closed-class words*. This can be seen as follows. Closed classes (such as prepositions) usually contain considerably fewer words than open classes (such as nouns). This means that a subtree rooted with a closed-class category tends to have a higher probability than a subtree rooted with an open-class category, since the probability of a subtree is calculated as the frequency of that subtree divided by the frequency of all subtrees with the same root category. For instance, an arbitrary P-subtree will tend to have a higher substitution probability than an arbitrary N-subtree. Other things being equal, this means that a parse tends to get a higher probability if its subtrees do *not* mismatch with a closed-class word, but with an open-class word.

This property represents an important result, as closed-class words rarely constitute problematic cases in parsing sentences. Note that in DOP3, it is not impossible to generalize over closed-class words, but it will only occur if no parse can be found by generalizing over other words.

As an example, consider again the ATIS sentence *Return to first inquiry*. This sentence can be parsed by mismatching *return* with a V-subtree (i.e. with a verb). But the sentence can also be parsed if *to* instead of *return* mismatches with a verb. Both cases imply exactly one mismatch with one V-subtree. However, the latter case implies a mismatch with a closed-class word, whose P-subtree has a relatively high probability. Thus, the mismatch with *return* is preferred, which yields the generation of the appropriate parse.

6 Experiments with DOP3

Treating all words as possible unknown-category words would certainly lead to an impractically large number of subtrees in the derivation forest. As we have seen, the set of possible NP-subtrees (of maximal depth three) consists of about 10^9 types, which is a factor 12000 larger than the set of observed NP-subtrees. It is therefore evident that we will get impractical processing times with DOP3.

If we still want to perform experiments with DOP3, we need to limit the mismatches as much as possible. It seems reasonable to allow the mismatches only for unknown words, and for a restricted set of potentially unknown-category words. From the ATIS training set we derive that only nouns and verbs are actually lexically ambiguous. In our experiments, we will therefore limit the potentially unknown-category words of an input sentence to the nouns and verbs. This means that only the words of the test sentence which are unknown in the training set or which are tagged as a noun or a verb in the training set are allowed to mismatch with subtree-terminals.

We used the same 90%/10% division of the ATIS corpus as in the previous chapter. To study experimentally the merits of DOP3, we distinguished two classes of test sentences:

1. test sentences containing both unknown and unknown-category words (26)
2. test sentences containing only unknown-category words (49)

Thus all 75 test sentences contained at least one potentially unknown-category word (verb or noun). The following table shows the results for subtree-depth ≤ 3.

test sentences	parse accuracy
with unknown words and unknown-category words	62% (16 out of 26)
with only unknown-category words	86% (42 out of 49)
all test sentences	77% (58 out of 75)

Table 7.2. Parse accuracy for word strings from the ATIS corpus by DOP3

The table shows that DOP3 has better performance than DOP2 in all respects (cf. table 6.1). The parse accuracy for the 26 sentences with unknown and unknown-category words at 62% is considerably higher than the 42% of DOP2. This corresponds to an increase of 5 correctly parsed sentences. For 3 of these 5 sentences, this is due to the correct parsing of unknown-category words, which DOP2 cannot handle anyway. There remain therefore two test sentences that show the actual merits of DOP3 with respect to unknown words: *What are the amenities?* and *What movies are scheduled for these flights?*.

Recall that DOP2 tagged, due to a bias for smaller subtrees, both *amenities* and *movies* incorrectly as singular nouns (NN), thus missing the agreement with the verb *are*. DOP3, on the other hand, correctly tags *amenities* and *movies* as plural nouns (NNS), thus maintaining the number agreement with *are*:

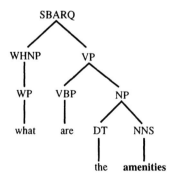

Figure 7.2. Most probable parse for *What are the amenities?*

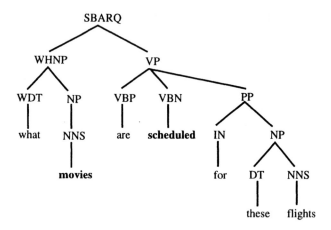

Figure 7.3. Most probable parse for *What **movies** are **scheduled** for these flights?*

We thus observe that the preference for parses that can be constructed out of the largest possible subtrees (containing agreement), and thus for parses that are most similar to previously seen analyses, has been recovered in DOP3 (cf. chapter 2).

Nevertheless, there are still 10 sentences with unknown words that are parsed incorrectly by DOP3. It is worth mentioning that for 8 of these sentences DOP3 generated *exactly* the same incorrect parses as DOP2 did, for instance as in figures 7.4 and 7.5. We conjecture that these sentences can only be parsed correctly if the ATIS annotations also contain morphological structure.

As to the sentences with only unknown-category words, the improvement of DOP3 with respect to DOP2 is equally impressive: the accuracy increased from 73% to 86%. However, the comparison with DOP2 may not be fair, as DOP2 cannot deal with unknown-category words at all.

There is an important question as to whether the success of DOP3 depends on the sophisticated Good-Turing method, or only on the assignment of very low probabilities to unknown subtrees. Despite the nice statistical justification of Good-Turing, we could ask whether we can achieve the same results if we simply assign a probability to unknown

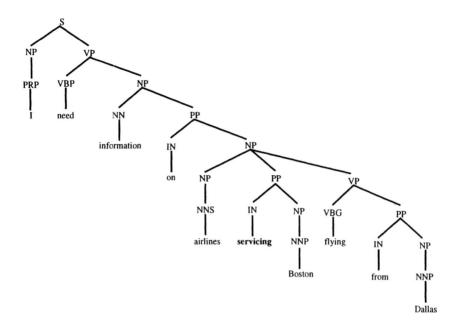

Figure 7.4. Incorrect most probable parse for the sentence *I need information on airlines **servicing** Boston flying from Dallas.*

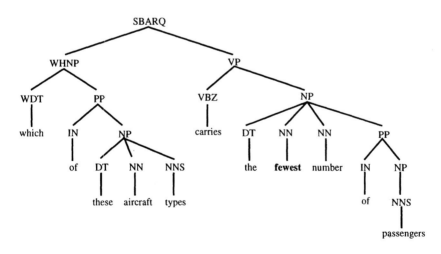

Figure 7.5. Incorrect most probable parse for *Which of these aircraft types carries the **fewest** number of passengers?*

subtrees which is (much) lower than the probabilities of known subtrees. A method which accomplishes this is the so-called *Add-k* method (Johnson 1932, Jeffreys 1948), which is often used in engineering practice. However, in Bod (1995b) it is shown that this method leads to worse results than the Good-Turing method for DOP. Moreover, the Add-k method is not founded on a statistical basis, whereas the Good-Turing method is.

8

An experience-based model for compositional semantic representations

So far, we have only dealt with the syntactic dimension of language performance. A syntactically analyzed corpus alone can never stand for a person's past language experience. In this chapter, we investigate what is involved in extending DOP to semantic interpretation. We will also go into the influence of recency and discourse structure.

1 Incorporating semantic interpretation

We consider the problem of computing the semantic interpretation of an input sentence that should be considered the most probable one on the basis of the frequencies of the interpretations of earlier sentences in a corpus. (We leave aside yet the influence of world knowledge and discourse context on the probability of interpretations.) A DOP model for semantic interpretation may be developed along the lines of the DOP models for syntactic analysis, employing a corpus of sentences with annotations that contain semantic as well as syntactic information. The decision about the semantic representation formalism is to some extent arbitrary, as long as this formalism has a well-defined model theory and is rich enough for representing the meanings of sentences and con-stituents that are relevant for the domain. In this chapter we will use a well-known standard formalism: extensional type theory (see Gamut 1991), i.e., a higher-order logical language that combines lambda-abstraction with connectives and quantifiers.

The rest of this section is divided into three parts. In subsection 1.1 we assume that every node in the syntactic constituent structure is annotated with a logical formula expressing its meaning, and that this meaning is derived compositionally from the meanings of its subconstituents. In subsection 1.2, we investigate the consequences of dropping this assumption. Finally, in subsection 1.3, we go into the probability model.

1.1 Assuming surface compositionality

If we are prepared to assume strict surface compositionality in the semantic annotation of the corpus trees, the corpus-based approach to the parsing problem generalizes in a straightforward way to the problem of computing semantic interpretations. By surface compositionality we mean that the way in which the semantics of a surface constituent X correlates with the semantics of the subconstituents of X can be explicitly indicated: the meaning of X can be specified by a logical expression which contains the meaning representations of the immediate sub-constituents of X as sub-expressions. If this situation consistently applies, we can annotate the corpus trees by (1) specifying for every terminal node a logical formula representing its meaning, and (2) specifying for every nonterminal node a formula schema which indicates how its meaning representation may be put together out of the formulas assigned to its daughter nodes. (In the examples below, these schemata use the variable $d1$ to indicate the meaning of the leftmost daughter constituent, $d2$ to indicate the meaning of the second daughter constituent, etc.)

Consider a corpus consisting of two very simple sentences, which is annotated in this way, in the following figure.

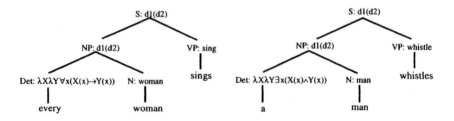

Figure 8.1. A corpus of two trees with syntactic and semantic labels

As in the purely syntactic DOP models, we now want to compute the probability of an analysis by considering all the different ways in which it can be generated by combining subtrees from the corpus. We can do this in virtually the same way. The only novelty is a slight modification in the process by which a corpus tree is decomposed into subtrees, and a corresponding modification in the composition operation which combines subtrees. If we extract a subtree out of a tree, we replace the semantics of the new frontier node with a unification variable of the same type. Correspondingly, when the composition operation substitutes a subtree at this node, this unification variable is unified with the semantic formula on the substituting tree. (It is required that the semantic type of this formula matches the semantic type of the unification variable.)

A simple example will make this clear. As before, we may try to analyze a sentence like *a woman whistles* by combining subtrees from the corpus. Consider the annotated corpus sentence *a man whistles* from this point of view. One of the relevant decompositions is the following one:

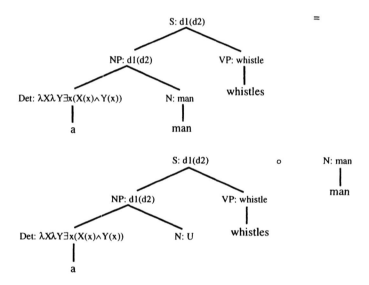

Figure 8.2. Decomposing a tree into subtrees with unification variables

We see that by decomposing the tree into two subtrees, the semantics at the breakpoint-node *N: man* is replaced by a variable. Now we can generate an analysis for the sentence *a woman whistles* in the following way.

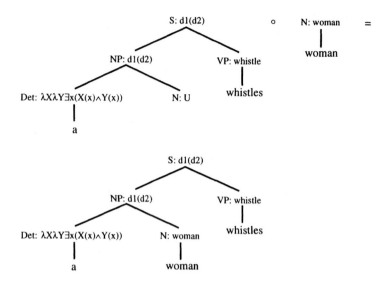

Figure 8.3. Generating an analysis for *A woman whistles*

If we would be happy to work with corpora with complete and compositional semantic annotations, we could leave it at that. However, the possibility of annotating large corpora of actually occurring text in this way may be called into question. And it seems that our approach might still work under somewhat less restricted conditions. It is worthwhile, therefore, to explore what happens when we loosen our assumptions about the nature of the semantic annotations.

As a first step, we consider the case where the semantics of the corpus trees and the input sentences *is* in fact compositional, but where we are using an annotation system which does not explicitly presuppose and exploit this. We go through the same simple example, but assuming a different annotation regime. Thus, consider again a corpus consisting of the same sentences as in figure 8.1, but now with the following annotation: every constituent carries a label that consists of a syntactic category and a logical formula representing the meaning of the constituent (figure 8.4).

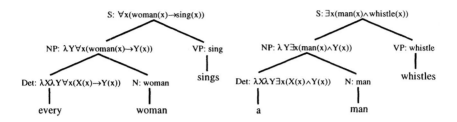

Figure 8.4. A corpus of two trees with syntactic and semantic labels consisting of logical formula

Again, we want to compute the probability of an analysis by considering all the different ways in which it can be generated by combining subtrees from the corpus. But decomposing the corpus trees into subtrees is a bit more complex now. This is due to the fact that possible dependencies between the semantic annotations of different nodes are not explicitly indicated now, while they may be strongly suggested by the fact that the formulas on these nodes contain the same descriptive constants.

To deal with this issue, the decomposition process by which subtrees are derived from the initial corpus of trees, may now be further refined as follows. If we extract a subtree out of a tree, we replace the semantics of the new frontier node with a unification variable (of the same type), and introduce this unification variable at every place where the semantics of this subtree appears in the labels of its governing nodes. The same example discussed before may serve to illustrate this.

Again, we try to analyze the sentence *a woman whistles* by combining subtrees from the corpus. Consider the annotated corpus sentence *a man whistles*. One of the relevant decompositions is the following:

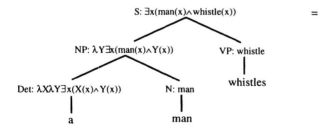

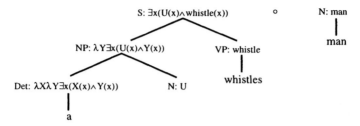

Figure 8.5. Decomposing a tree into subtrees with unification variables

We see that by decomposing the tree into two subtrees, the semantics at the breakpoint-node *N: man* is abstracted out of this label and out of the meanings of its governing constituents by replacing it with a variable. If we want to compose these two subtrees again, we need to enrich our composition operation with a unification mechanism: the meaning of the substituted subtree is unified with the variable in the label on which this subtree was substituted, and with the corresponding variables in the governing labels. Having this new combination operation and our abstraction mechanism, we can generate an analysis for the sentence *a woman whistles* in the following way.

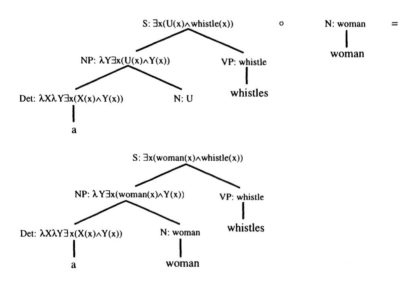

Figure 8.6. Generating an analysis for *a woman whistles* with abstraction and unification

Of course, this example was unrealistically simple. It may often happen that the logical expression representing the meaning of a constituent is not literally present in the meaning representations of the larger constituents that contain it. In such cases the meaning of a subtree cannot be abstracted directly out of the formulas on its governing nodes. However, if we in fact assume surface compositionality, the class of expressions *equivalent* to the formula on a certain governing node, will always contain expressions in which the semantics of a subordinate constituent *does* literally (and non-trivially) appear. Let us consider the following tree again:

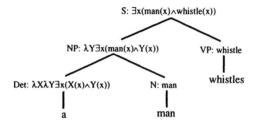

Figure 8.7. Example tree

We note that the representation of the meaning of the NP *a man*, which is $\lambda Y \exists x(man(x) \wedge Y(x))$, is not literally present in the logical expression at the S node, which is $\exists x(man(x) \wedge whistle(x))$. However, in the class of expressions equivalent to $\exists x(man(x) \wedge whistle(x))$, there is the expression $\lambda Y \exists x(man(x) \wedge Y(x))$ (*whistle*) out of which the expression $\lambda Y \exists x(man(x) \wedge Y(x))$ can be directly abstracted, yielding $U(whistle)$. Assuming an algorithm for computing equivalent expressions, we may thus be able to decompose the above tree into the following subtrees:

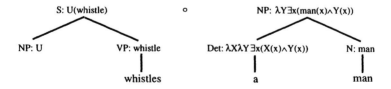

Figure 8.8. Decomposing the tree in figure 8.7 into two subtrees by using equivalence relations

And we can now parse the sentence *every woman whistles* by combining the following subtrees from the corpus.

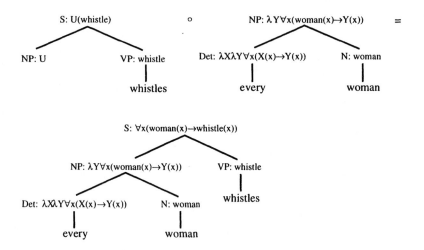

Figure 8.9. Parsing the sentence *every woman whistles*

It is perhaps trivial to note that, analogous to the syntactic DOP models, a tree can be decomposed also into more than two subtrees, as is illustrated in figure 8.10.

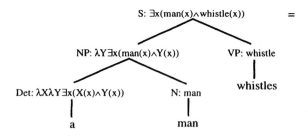

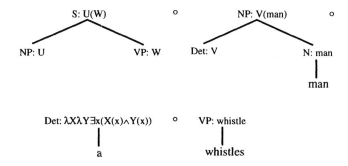

Figure 8.10. A tree can be decomposed into several subtrees

We have thus seen that it is not impossible to work with a corpus that is annotated in a way which downplays surface compositionality in that constituents are labeled with fully instantiated semantic representations, rather than with definitions that refer to the semantics of their sub-constituents. We have also seen that there may be a certain cost: this approach may give rise to substantial amounts of equivalence calculations on complex lambda-expressions.

In passing we also mention another problem that did not occur in our initial, explicitly compositional, approach. When we label nodes with full semantic representations, there is no explicit information about how these representations were built up (or should be imagined to have been built up). Therefore, when a subtree is extracted out and the corresponding semantic abstraction takes place, it is not always uniquely defined which parts of a formula must be replaced by the unification variable. A simple example is the sentence *Every man loves a man.* If one of the occurrences of *man* is abstracted out, it is not formally defined what replacements must be made in the formula at the S-node. Whether this kind of problem is statistically significant is not clear, however. (Every sentence-analysis process involves many different trees from the corpus, and most of these will not give rise to such confusions.)

Acknowledging these disadvantages, we nevertheless remain interested in the idea of annotating the nodes of the trees with full semantic representations rather than with compositional definitions. One reason is that we are ultimately pessimistic about the feasibility of that kind of annotation for large corpora of actual text. Another reason is, that full-representation-annotation is more easily compatible with the idea of *partial* annotations.

1.2 Not assuming surface compositionality: partial annotations

We now explore some situations where an initial, intuitively assigned annotation may be expected to be incomplete. One such situation is the phenomenon of non-standard quantifier scope. We illustrate this phenomenon with a well-known example sentence.

Suppose that the sentence *Every man loves a woman* occurs in a (larger) corpus with the following annotation (which in the context in which it was uttered was for some reason the most appropriate one for interpreting the utterance). The annotation gives the semantics of subconstituents only in so far as a meaning that can be locally established can also be straightforwardly recognized in the semantics of the total utterance.

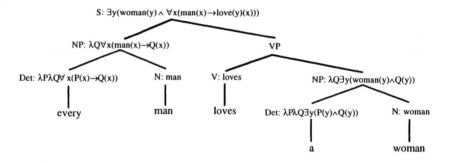

Figure 8.11. Partial annotation for the sentence *Every man loves a woman*

The semantics of the whole utterance is known, as well as the semantics of the NPs *every man* and *a woman*. Also the interpretation of the verb *loves* is straightforward, but the semantics of the VP *loves a woman* is left unspecified, since the semantics that one would intuitively assign to this phrase does not occur as a sub-expression of the semantics of the complete utterance. Nevertheless, we do not want to exclude that subtrees headed by this VP node are employed as structural/semantic units in the parsing process. When, for this reason, the meaning of this VP is needed anyway, it can be arrived at by lambda-abstracting out the contribution of the VP's sister node from the semantics of the mother node.

To arrive at the meaning of the VP constituent *loves a woman*, the system must abstract out the meaning of the NP *every man*, i.e. $\lambda Q \forall x(man(x) \rightarrow Q(x))$, from the meaning of the whole sentence, i.e. $\exists y(woman(y) \wedge \forall x(man(x) \rightarrow love(y)(x)))$. To make this possible, the meaning of the whole sentence must first be paraphrased as $\exists y(woman(y) \wedge \lambda Q \forall x(man(x) \rightarrow Q(x)) (love(y)))$. Then, the NP-semantics $\lambda Q \forall x(man(x) \rightarrow Q(x))$ can be λ-abstracted straightforwardly out of the sentence-semantics, yielding $\lambda P \exists y(woman(y) \wedge P(love(y)))$.

Clearly, this treatment is reminiscent of the type-lifting rules of "Flexible Montague Grammar" (Hendriks 1993). But since we are not writing a grammar but designing a performance model that works off semantically annotated trees, our treatment is a kind of mirror-image of the Flexible Montague Grammar approach. In our system, we start with the semantics of the full sentence, however complex or non-standard it may be. Like Flexible Montague Grammar, we then exploit the power of the lambda-calculus to enforce a compositional construction of that sentence semantics.

We expect that it is not realistic to assume that corpora are completely annotated. Partial annotations seem more appropriate because of phenomena like non-standard scope orders (like the example above), idioms, and discontinuous constituents. In a partially annotated corpus, meanings of nodes are not necessarily specified. For a sentence to count as analyzed and understood, what needs to be stored is (1) its syntactic structure and (2) its meaning.

Therefore, the only semantic feature on the tree that is necessarily specified is the one at the top; the meanings of subconstituents may or may not be specified. But subtrees will only be useful for the semantic analysis of new input utterances, to the extent that their meanings are either explicitly specified or formally derivable. The meaning of a constituent is derivable either by simple composition of the meanings of its subordinate constituents, or by abstracting out the contribution(s) of its sister node(s) in the semantics of its mother node.

An extreme case of a partial annotation may be provided by certain idioms. If we are given the sentence *John kicked the bucket* and are aware that this means that John died, we have the following structure in figure 8.12 with semantic annotation *die(john)*. If we add to this the knowledge that *John* is annotated with *john*, we can derive a meaning for the VP, but not further down.

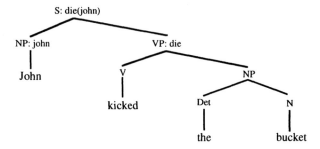

Figure 8.12. Partial annotation for the sentence *John kicked the bucket*

This effectively means that semantically, but not syntactically, the whole idiomatic phrase *kicked the bucket* is treated as one word.

Another phenomenon that may give rise to partial annotations is provided by certain kinds of discontinuous constituency. Consider the following annotation of the sentence *de Kerstman tuigde de kerstboom op* (i.e. *Santa Claus decorated the X-mas tree*).

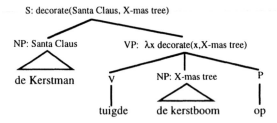

Figure 8.13. Partial annotation for the sentence *de Kerstman tuigde de kerstboom op*

Again, the semantics at a node is specified only in so far as a meaning that can be locally established can also be straightforwardly recognized in the semantics of the total utterance. Thus, besides the meaning of the whole utterance, only the meanings of the NPs *de Kerstman* and *de kerstboom* and the meaning of the VP *tuigde de kerstboom op* are specified. The separate meanings of *tuigde* and *op* can neither be established locally, nor can they be arrived at by abstraction. However, the meaning of *tuigde* and *op* together can be established by decomposing the VP *tuigde de kerstboom op* into subtrees, i.e. by abstracting out the NP *de kerstboom*:

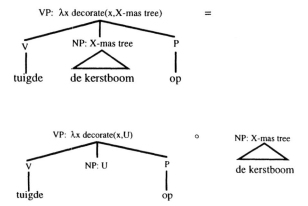

Figure 8.14. Deriving structure and semantics for the discontinuous constituent *tuigde op*

Thus, the discontinuous constituent *tuigde op* can be used as a productive structural unit, also if it is separated by an NP.

In this semantic DOP model, any subtree can function as a productive unit, even if its semantics is not yet completely specified, provided its semantics can be calculated in the end by employing the Principle of Compositionality of Meaning in one of two ways: (1) the meaning is constructed by simple composition of the constituents or (2) the meaning is arrived at by abstracting out the contribution(s) of the sister node(s) from the semantics of the node directly governing it.

1.3   The probability model of semantic DOP

We now define the probability of a meaning of a string on the basis of a semantically annotated corpus.

Given a partially annotated corpus as defined above, the multiset of corpus subtrees consists of all subtrees with a well-defined top-node semantics, that are generated by applying to the trees of the corpus the decomposition mechanism described above. The probability of substituting a subtree t on a specific node is the probability of selecting t among all subtrees in the multiset that could be substituted on that node. Analogous to DOP1, this probability is equal to the number of occurrences of a subtree t, divided by the total number of occurrences of subtrees t' with the same root node category as t (where a root node category of a subtree is now identified by its syntactic label and the type of its semantic formula -- see § 1.2):

$$P(t) = \frac{|t|}{\sum_{t':\, r(t')=r(t)} |t'|}$$

A derivation of a string is a tuple of subtrees, such that their composition results in a tree whose yield is the string. The probability of a derivation $D = t_1 \circ ... \circ t_n$ is the product of the probabilities of these subtrees:

$$P(t_1 \circ ... \circ t_n) = \prod_i P(t_i)$$

A tree resulting from a derivation of a string is called a parse tree of this string. The probability of a parse tree T is the probability that it is produced by any of its derivations D; this is the sum of the probabilities of all its derivations:

$$P(T) = \sum_{D \text{ derives } T} P(D)$$

A meaning of a string is a formula which is logically equivalent to the semantic annotation of the top node of a parse of this string. The probability of a meaning M is the sum of the probabilities of the parses with a top node annotated with a formula that is logically equivalent to M:

$$P(M) = \sum_{T \text{ has meaning } M} P(T)$$

Note that this probability model allows us to formally relate language comprehension and language production (see chapter 1). In language comprehension we are interested in the most probable meaning M for a given word string W, which is written as: $\text{argmax}_M P(M \mid W)$, while in language production we are interested in the most probable word string W for a given meaning M, written as: $\text{argmax}_W P(W \mid M)$.

2 Extending DOP to discourse and recency

In all DOP models defined so far, we have assumed that the recency of previous language experiences does not influence the analysis of a sentence. For the ATIS corpus, this assumption may be close to true, as this corpus merely contains distinct questions and imperatives without discourse structure. A sentence like *Show me the flights from Boston to New York early in the morning* can be properly interpreted by taking into account only the frequencies of previous sub-analyses.

It is well-known, however, that not only the frequency but also the *recency* of previous experiences bias the analysis of a new utterances (e.g. Bock 1986; Gibson 1990; Kempen 1996). A reason for this may be the impact of human memory limitations, but the impact of discourse structure may be even stronger. Consider the following two contiguous sentences:

> *I see a man with a dog*
> *And I see a man with a telescope*

It is clear that, due to the phenomenon of *parallelism*, the analysis of the first sentence creates a very strong bias in analyzing the second sentence. A performance model which wants to take this phenomenon into account should not only register all previous analyses but should also order them in time of occurrence.

If we limit ourselves for the moment to local discourse structure, how can we integrate the notion of recency into the DOP framework? We conjecture that recency can and should be integrated into the statistics of the performance model. It is interesting to note that there is some support for this conjecture: psycholinguistic experiments indicate that there is a close connection between recency and frequency. For example, Bock (1986: 380) shows that the recent perception or production of a particular structure increases its probability of being used relative to other structures. This finding supports the idea that recency should not be treated as a separate component in the DOP framework, but as part of the probability model. Recency may be described by a function which adjusts the frequencies of occurrence of analyses in such a way that the frequencies of more recently perceived/produced fragments are adjusted upwards and those of less recently perceived/produced fragments are adjusted downwards, possibly down to zero. This means that analysis fragments may be forgotten if they are not perceived or produced again.[10]

As to the quantitative definition of recency, psychologists have suggested many functions to describe the monotonic loss of information with time, ranging from linear, hyperbolic, exponential and logarithmic functions (see Rubin & Wenzel 1996 for an overview). We will not go into the question as to which of these functions is most adequate for DOP; rather we want to emphasize that none of the proposed functions does justice to the *hierarchical* structure of discourse (Polanyi 1985; Scha & Polanyi 1988). Consider the following sentences.

> *I see a man with a dog*
> *Look how old he is!*
> *He must be at least eighty*
> *He hits the dog with a stick*
> *And there I see a man with a telescope*

In this piece of discourse, the perceived analysis of the last sentence is strongly influenced by the analysis of the first sentence, and not by the analyses of the sentences in between, regardless the fact that they are more recent. Thus, recency is *not* a monotonically decreasing function, but a discontinuous recursive function which closely follows the resursive structure of the discourse. In coordinated pieces of discourse, recency may be indeed monotonically decreasing, but as soon as a subordinated discourse unit comes in, the current recency function is put on a stack and a new recency function is triggered. After the subordinated piece of discourse is closed, the previous recency function is taken from the stack again, and is used as the current one.

For DOP this means that a corpus should not be represented as a contiguous set of trees, but as a tree of trees, where each syntactic/ semantic sentence-analysis is a node in a complex hierarchical discourse structure. Unfortunately, such corpora do not (yet) exist. What do exist are simple dialogue corpora of question-answer pairs that are annotated with semantic annotations as explained in the previous section. An

---

[10] That the persistence of fragments in human memory is nevertheless remarkable may be illustrated by the fact that in reading Marcel Proust's magnum opus *A la Recherche du Temps Perdu*, one is able to notice that this seven volume work begins and ends with the same words.

example of such a corpus is the OVIS ("Openbaar Vervoer Informatie Systeem") corpus. On the basis of this corpus, recency and discourse can be straightforwardly modeled by interpreting a new utterance in the context of its immediately preceding dialogue. This will be one of the topics of the next chapter.

9

Speech understanding and dialogue processing

In this chapter we show how the semantic DOP model can be used for computing the interpretation of spoken input in a practical dialogue system called OVIS. OVIS, Openbaar Vervoer Informatie Systeem ("Public Transport Information System"), is a Dutch spoken language information system which operates over ordinary telephone lines. The prototype system is the immediate goal of the NWO[11] Priority Programme "Language and Speech Technology".

We first give a description of the OVIS corpus, after which we show how this corpus can be used by the semantic DOP model to compute the most likely meaning of a word string. We then demonstrate how the dialogue context can be integrated into the model, and how DOP can be interfaced with speech. The experiments we accomplish on the OVIS corpus reinforce the properties that were derived in chapter 5 for the ATIS corpus.

1 The OVIS corpus: trees enriched with compositional frame semantics

The OVIS corpus currently consists of 10,000 syntactically and semantically annotated user utterances that were collected on the basis of a pilot version of the OVIS system[12]. The user utterances are answers to system questions such as *From where to where do you want to travel?, At what time do you want to travel from Utrecht to Leiden?, Could you please repeat your destination?.*

---

[11] Netherlands Organization of Scientific Research.

[12] The pilot version is based on a German system developed by Philips Dialogue Systems in Aachen (Aust et al. 1995), adapted to Dutch.

For the syntactic annotation of the OVIS user utterances, a tag set of 40 lexical/syntactic categories was developed. This tag set was deliberately kept small so as to improve the robustness of the DOP parser. A correlate of this robustness is that the parser overgenerates, but as long as the probability model can accurately select the correct utterance-analysis from all possible analyses, overgeneration is not problematic. Robustness is further achieved by a special category, called ERROR. This category is used for stutters, false starts, and repairs (see figure 9.2). No grammar is used to determine the correct syntactic annotation; there is a small set of guidelines that has the degree of detail necessary to avoid an "anything goes" attitude in the annotator but leaves room for the annotator's perception of the structure of the utterance (see Bonnema et al. 1997).

The semantic annotations are based on the *update language* defined for the OVIS dialogue manager by Veldhuijzen van Zanten (1996). This language consists of a hierarchical frame structure with slots and values for the origin and destination of a train connection, for the time at which the user wants to arrive or depart, etc. The distinction between slots and values can be seen as a special case of ground and focus distinction (Vallduvi 1990). Updates specify the ground and focus of the user utterances. For example, the utterance *Ik wil niet vandaag maar morgen naar Almere* (literally: "*I want not today but tomorrow to Almere*") yields the following update:

```
user.wants.(([# today];[! tomorrow]);
            destination.place.town.almere)
```

An important property of this update language is that it allows encoding of speech-act information (cf. van Noord et al 1997). The "#" in the update means that the information between the square brackets (representing the focus of the user utterance) must be retracted, while the "!" represents the corrected information.

This update language is used to compositionally enrich the syntactic nodes of the OVIS trees with semantic annotations by means of the following annotation convention:

(1) Every meaningful *lexical* node is annotated with a slot and/or value from the update language which represents the meaning of the lexical item.

(2) Every meaningful *non-lexical* node is annotated with a *formula schema* which indicates how its meaning representation can be put together out of the meaning representations assigned to its daughter nodes.

In the examples below, these formula schemata use the variable *d1* to indicate the meaning of the leftmost daughter constituent, *d2* to indicate the meaning of the second daughter node constituent, etc (cf. chapter 8). For instance, the full (syntactic and semantic) annotation for the above sentence *Ik wil niet vandaag maar morgen naar Almere* is given in fig. 9.1.

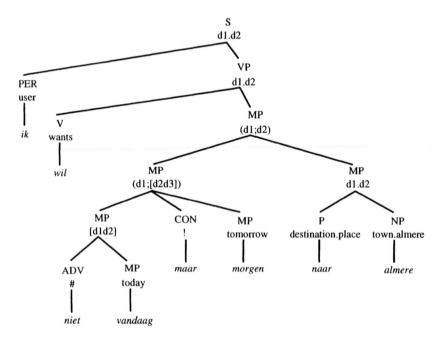

Figure 9.1. OVIS annotation for *Ik wil niet vandaag maar morgen naar Almere*

The meaning of *Ik wil niet vandaag maar morgen naar Almere* is thus compositionally built up out of the meanings of its subconstituents. Substituting the meaning representations into the corresponding variables yields the update semantics of the top-node: user.wants. ((([# today];[! tomorrow]);destination.place.town.almere).

Notice that our annotation convention is based on the notion of *surface compositionality*: it assumes that the meaning representation of a surface-constituent *can* in fact always be composed out of the meaning representations of its subconstituents. As we have seen in the previous chapter, this assumption is not unproblematic. To maintain it in the face of phenomena such as non-standard quantifier scope or discontinuous constituents creates complications in the syntactic or semantic analyses assigned to certain sentences and their constituents. It is unlikely therefore that our annotation convention can be viewed as completely general. However, by using the daughter notation, subtrees can be directly extracted out of the annotated trees and the same parsing and disambiguation algorithms can be used as designed for DOP1 (whereas the formula notation would require a procedure that inspects the semantic formula of a node in order to determine the contribution of the semantics of the other nodes -- see chapter 8). To the best of our knowledge, the OVIS is the first corpus annotated according to the Principle of Compositionality of Meaning (cf. Miller et al. 1996).

Figure 9.2 gives an example of the ERROR category for the annotation of the ill-formed sentence *Van Voorburg naar van Venlo naar Voorburg* (*"From Voorburg to from Venlo to Voorburg"*):

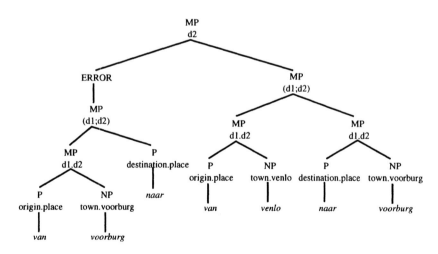

Figure 9.2. OVIS annotation for *Van Voorburg naar van Venlo naar Voorburg*

Note that the ERROR category has no semantic annotation; in the top-node semantics of *Van Voorburg naar van Venlo naar Voorburg* the meaning of the false start *Van Voorburg naar* is thus absent:

```
(origin.place.town.venlo ;
 destination.place.town.voorburg)
```

The manual annotation of 10,000 OVIS utterances may seem a laborious and error-prone process. In order to expedite this task, a flexible and powerful annotation workbench (SEMTAGS) was developed by Bonnema (1996). SEMTAGS is a graphical interface, written in C using the XVIEW toolkit. It offers all functionality needed for examining, evaluating, and editing syntactic and semantic analyses. SEMTAGS is mainly used for correcting the output of the DOP parser. After the first 100 OVIS utterances were annotated and checked by hand, the parser used the subtrees of the resulting annotations to produce analyses for the following 100 OVIS utterances. These new analyses were checked and corrected by the annotator using SEMTAGS, and were added to the total set of annotations. This new set of 200 annotations was then used by the DOP parser to predict the analyses for a next subset of OVIS utterances. In this incremental, bootstrapping way, 10,000 OVIS utterances were annotated in approximately 600 hours (supervision included).

2 Using the OVIS corpus for data-oriented semantic analysis

An important advantage of a corpus annotated on the basis of surface compositionality is that its subtrees can directly be used by DOP for computing syntactic/semantic representations for new utterances. The only difference is that we now have composite labels which do not only contain syntactic but also semantic information.

By way of illustration, we show how a representation for the input utterance *Ik wil van Venlo naar Almere* ("*I want from Venlo to Almere*") can be constructed out of subtrees from the trees in figures 9.1 and 9.2:

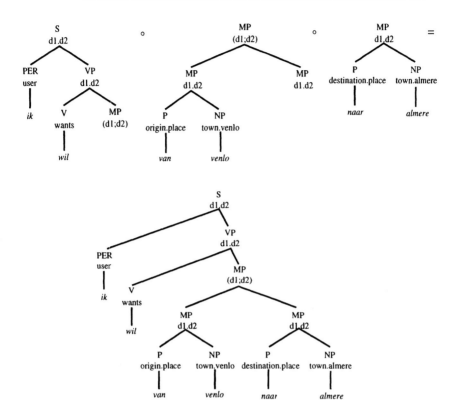

Figure 9.3. Derivation and analysis for *Ik wil van Venlo naar Almere*

which yields the following top-node update semantics:

```
user.wants.
        (origin.place.town.venlo;
        destination.place.town.almere)
```

The probability model for this semantic DOP model has been given in chapter 8. That is, the probability of a subtree t is equal to the number of occurrences of t in the corpus, divided by the total number of occurrences of subtrees t' that can be substituted on the same node as t. The probability of a derivation $D = t_1 \circ ... \circ t_n$ is the product of the probabilities of its subtrees t_i. The probability of a parse tree T is the sum of the probabilities of all derivations D that produce T. And the probability of a meaning M and a word string W is the sum of the probabilities of all parse trees T of W that have a top-node meaning which is logically equivalent to M.

As with the most probable parse, the most probable meaning cannot be computed in deterministic polynomial time, although it can be estimated by Monte Carlo sampling. Unfortunately, the computation of a sufficiently large number of random derivations is currently not efficient enough for a practical system. To date, only the *most probable derivation* can be computed in near-to-real-time (by Viterbi optimization -- see chapter 4). We will therefore assume that most of the probability mass for each top-node meaning is focussed on a single derivation. Under this assumption, the most likely meaning of a string is the top-node meaning generated by the most likely derivation of that string.

3 Extending DOP to dialogue context: context-dependent subcorpora

We now extend the semantic DOP model to compute the most likely meaning of a sentence given the previous dialogue. In general, the probability of a top-node meaning M and a particular word string W_i given an ongoing dialogue-context $C_i = W_{i-1}, W_{i-2} \dots W_1$ is given by $P(M, W_i \mid W_{i-1}, W_{i-2} \dots W_1)$.

Since the OVIS user utterances are typically answers to previous system questions, we assume that the meaning of a word string W_i does not depend on the full dialogue context but only on the previous (system) question W_{i-1}. Under this assumption,

$$P(M, W_i \mid C_i) \;=\; P(M, W_i \mid W_{i-1})$$

For DOP, this formula means that the update semantics of a user utterance W_i is computed on the basis of the subcorpus which contains all OVIS utterances (with their annotations) that are answers to the system question W_{i-1}. This gives rise to the following interesting model for dialogue processing: each system question triggers a context-dependent domain (a subcorpus) by which the user answer is analyzed and interpreted. Since the number of different system questions is a small closed set (see Veldhuijzen van Zanten 1996), we can create off-line for each subcorpus the corresponding DOP parser.

In OVIS, the following context-dependent subcorpora can be distinguished:

(1) place subcorpus: utterances following questions like *From where to where do you want to travel? What is your destination?*, etc.

(2) date subcorpus: utterances following questions like *When do you want to travel?, When do you want to leave from X?, When do you want to arrive in Y?*, etc.

(3) time subcorpus: utterances following questions like *At what time do you want to travel? At what time do you want to leave from X?, At what time do you want to arrive in Y?*, etc.

(4) yes/no subcorpus: utterances following y/n-questions like *Did you say that ...? Thus you want to arrive at ...?*

Note that a subcorpus can contain utterances whose topic goes beyond the previous system question. For example, if the system asks *From where to where do you want to travel?*, and the user answers with: *From Amsterdam to Groningen tomorrow morning*, then the date-expression *tomorrow morning* ends up in the place-subcorpus.

It is interesting to note that this context-sensitive DOP model can be easily extended to domain-dependent interpretation in general: a corpus is clustered into subcorpora, where each subcorpus corresponds to a topic-dependent domain. A new utterance is interpreted by the domain in which it gets highest probability. Since small subcorpora tend to assign higher probabilities to an utterance than large subcorpora (because the relative frequencies of the subtrees in small corpora are higher), it follows that a language user strives for the smallest, most specific domain in which the perceived utterance can still be analyzed, thus establishing a most specific common ground.

4 Interfacing DOP with speech

So far, we have dealt with the estimation of the probability $P(M, W \mid C)$ of a meaning M and a word string W given a dialogue context C. However, in *spoken* dialogue processing, the word string W is not given. The input to DOP in the OVIS system are *word-graphs* produced by the speech recognizer (these word-graphs are generated by our project partners from the University of Nijmegen -- see Boves et al. 1996).

A word-graph is a compact representation for all sequences of words that the speech recognizer hypothesizes for an acoustic utterance A (see figure 9.4). The nodes of the graph represent points in time, and a transition between two nodes i and j represents a word w that may have been uttered between the corresponding points in time. For convenience we refer to transitions in the word-graph using the notation $<i, j, w>$. The word-graphs are optimized to eliminate *epsilon* transitions. Such transitions represent periods of time when the speech recognizer hypothesizes that no words are uttered. Each transition is associated with an acoustic score. This is the negative logarithm (of base 10) of the acoustic probability $P(a \mid w)$ for a hypothesized word w normalized by the length of w. By converting the acoustic scores into their corresponding probabilities, the acoustic probability $P(A \mid W)$ for a hypothesized word string W can be computed by the product of the acoustic probabilities of the transitions in the corresponding word-graph path. Figure 9.4 shows an example of a simplified word-graph for the uttered sentence *Ik wil graag vanmorgen naar Leiden* ("*I'd like to go this morning to Leiden*"):

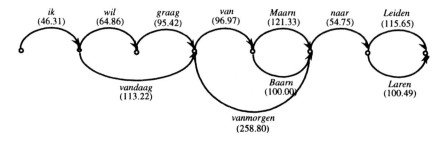

Figure 9.4. Simplified word-graph for the acoustic utterance *Ik wil graag vanmorgen naar Leiden*

The probabilistic interface between DOP and speech word-graphs thus consists of the interface between the DOP probabilities $P(M, W \mid C)$ and the word-graph probabilities $P(A \mid W)$ so as to compute the probability $P(M, A \mid C)$ and $\text{argmax}_M P(M, A \mid C)$. We start by rewriting $P(M, A \mid C)$ as:

$$P(M, A \mid C) \ = \ \Sigma_W \ P(M, W, A \mid C)$$
$$= \ \Sigma_W \ P(M, W \mid C) \cdot P(A \mid M, W, C)$$

The first factor $P(M, W \mid C)$ corresponds to the probability computed by the dialogue-sensitive DOP model as explained in the previous section. To estimate the probability $P(A \mid M, W, C)$ on the basis of the information available in a word-graph, we must make the following independence assumption: the acoustic utterance A depends only on the word string W, and not on its context C and meaning M (cf. Bod & Scha 1994). Under this assumption:

$$P(M, A \mid C) \ = \ \Sigma_W \ P(M, W \mid C) \cdot P(A \mid W)$$

To make fast computation feasible, we furthermore assume that most of the probability mass for each meaning and acoustic utterance is focused on a single word string W (this will allow for efficient Viterbi best first search):

$$P(M, A \mid C) \ = \ P(M, W \mid C) \cdot P(A \mid W)$$

Thus, the probability of a meaning M for an acoustic utterance A given a context C is computed by the product of the DOP probability $P(M, W \mid C)$ and the word-graph probability $P(A \mid W)$.

As to the parsing of word-graphs, it is well-known that parsing algorithms for word strings can easily be generalized to word-graphs (e.g. van Noord 1995). For word strings, the initialization of the chart usually consists of entering each word w_i into chart entry $<i, i+1>$. For word-graphs, a transition $<i, j, w>$ corresponds to a word w between positions i and j where j is not necessarily equal to $i+1$ (see figure 9.4). It is easy to see that for word-graphs the initialization of the chart consists of entering each word w from transition $<i, j, w>$ into chart entry $<i, j>$. Next, parsing proceeds with the subtrees that are triggered by the dialogue context C (provided that all subtrees are converted into rewrite rules -- see chapter 4). The most likely derivation is computed by a bottom-up chart parser using Viterbi optimization (Sima'an 1996a). This parser runs with a worst case time complexity which is cubic in the number of word-graph nodes and linear in the grammar size. The top-node meaning of the tree produced by the most likely derivation is taken as the best meaning *M* for an utterance *A* given context *C*.

5 Experiments

In our experimental evaluation we were interested in the following questions:

(1) Is DOP fast enough for practical spoken dialogue understanding?
(2) Can we constrain the OVIS subtrees without loosing accuracy?
(3) What is the impact of dialogue context on accuracy?

For all experiments, we used a random split of the 10,000 OVIS trees into a 90% training set and a 10% test set. The training set was divided up into the four subcorpora given in section 4, which were used to create the corresponding DOP parsers. The 1000 word-graphs corresponding to the test set utterances were used as input. For each word-graph, the previous system question was known to determine the particular DOP parser. As to the complexity of the word-graphs: the average number of transitions per word is 4.2, and the average number of words per word-graph path is 4.6. All experiments were run on a Silicon Graphics *Indigo* with a MIPS R10000 processor and 640 Mbyte of core memory.

To establish the semantic accuracy of the system, the best meanings produced by the DOP parser were compared with the meanings in the test set. Besides an exact match metric, we also used a more fine-grained evaluation for the semantic accuracy. Following the proposals in Boros et al. (1996) and van Noord et al. (1997), we translated each *update* meaning into a set of *semantic units*, where a unit is triple <CommunicativeFunction, Slot, Value>. For instance, the next example

```
user.wants.travel.destination.
                ([# place.town.almere];
                [! place.town.alkmaar])
```
translates as:

```
<denial, destination_town, almere>
<correction, destination_town, alkmaar>
```

Both the updates in the OVIS test set and the updates produced by the DOP parser were translated into semantic units of the form given above. The semantic accuracy was then evaluated in three different ways: (1) *match*, the percentage of updates which were exactly correct (i.e., which exactly matched the updates in the test set); (2) *precision*, the number of correct semantic units divided by the number of semantic units which were produced; (3) *recall*, the number of correct semantic units divided by the number of semantic units in the test set.

As to question (1), we already suspect that it is not efficient to use *all* OVIS subtrees. As in chapters 5 and 6, we perform experiments with versions of DOP where the subtree collection is restricted to subtrees with a certain maximum depth. The following table shows for four different maximum depths (where the maximum number of frontier words is limited to 3), the number of subtree types in the training set, the semantic accuracy in terms of match, precision and recall (in percentages), and the average CPU time per word-graph in seconds.

subtree-depth	#subtrees	semantic accuracy			CPU time
		match	precision	recall	
1	3191	76.2	79.4	82.1	0.21
2	10545	78.5	83.0	84.3	0.86
3	32140	79.8	84.7	86.2	2.76
4	64486	80.6	85.8	86.9	6.03

Table 9.1. Experimental results on OVIS word-graphs

The experiments show that at subtree-depth 4 the highest accuracy is achieved, but that only for subtree-depths 1 and 2 are the processing times fast enough for a practical application.[13] Thus there is a trade-off between efficiency and accuracy: the efficiency deteriorates if the accuracy improves. We believe that a match of 78.5% and a corresponding precision and recall of resp. 83.0% and 84.3% (for the fast

---

[13] We want to mention that for subtrees larger than depth 4, the semantic accuracy did not increase any further (see also Bonnema et al. 1997). This may be due to the fact that the average number of words per word-graph path is only 4.6 in the OVIS domain.

processing times at depth 2) is promising enough for further research. Moreover, by testing DOP directly on the word strings (without the word-graphs), a match of 97.8% was achieved. This shows that linguistic ambiguities do not play a significant role in this domain. The actual problem are the ambiguities in the word-graphs (i.e. the multiple paths).

Secondly, we are concerned with the question as to whether we can impose constraints on the subtrees other than their depth, in such a way that the accuracy does not deteriorate and perhaps even improves. To answer this question, we kept the maximal subtree-depth constant at 3, and employed the following constraints:

- *Restricting subtree lexicalization*: restricting the maximum number of words in the subtree frontiers to resp. 3, 2 and 1, showed a decrease in semantic accuracy similar to the decrease in parse accuracy for the ATIS corpus in table 5.2. The *match* dropped from 79.8% to 76.9% if each subtree was lexicalized with only one word.

- *Eliminating once-occurring subtrees*: this led to a decrease in accuracy for all metrics; e.g. *match* decreased from 79.8% to 75.5%.

- *Eliminating subtrees with only non-head words*: this led also to a decrease in accuracy; the most stringent metric decreased from 79.8% to 77.1%. Evidently, there can be important relations in OVIS that involve non-head words.

These results indicate that the properties that were derived for the syntactically annotated (English) ATIS corpus in chapter 5 receive further support from the semantically annotated (Dutch) OVIS corpus.

Finally, we are interested in the impact of dialogue context on semantic accuracy. To test this, we neglected the previous system questions and created one DOP parser for the whole training set. The semantic accuracy metric *match* dropped from 79.8% to 77.4% (for depth 3). Moreover, the CPU time per sentence deteriorated by a factor of 4 (which is mainly due to the fact that larger training sets yield slower DOP parsers).

The following result nicely illustrates how the dialogue context can contribute to better predictions for the correct meaning of an utterance. In parsing the word-graph corresponding to the acoustic utterance *Donderdag acht februari* ("*Thursday eight February*"), the DOP model without dialogue context assigned highest probability to the word string *Dordrecht acht februari* and its corresponding meaning. The uttered word *Donderdag* was thus interpreted as the town *Dordrecht* which was among the other hypothesized words in the word-graph. If the DOP model took into account the dialogue context, the previous system question *When do you want to leave?* was known and triggered the subtrees from the date-subcorpus only, which now correctly assigned the highest probability to *Donderdag acht februari* and its meaning rather than to *Dordrecht acht februari*.

Note that this DOP model for speech and dialogue processing can still be improved. The OVIS utterances can be enriched with discourse annotations, such as co-reference links, in order to cope with anaphora resolution. The annotations can furthermore be extended with feature structures and/or functional structures associated with the surface structures so as to deal with more complex linguistic phenomena (see next chapter). What we have shown in this chapter, is, that DOP can be used for fast context-sensitive interpretation of spoken input in a practical dialogue system, and that the properties derived for the syntactic DOP model are reinforced for this semantic spoken dialogue DOP model.

10

Experience-based models for non-context-free representations

with Ronald Kaplan

It is well-known that there exist many syntactic and semantic dependencies that are not reflected directly in a surface tree. All modern linguistic theories propose more articulated representations and mechanisms in order to characterize such linguistic phenomena. DOP models for context-free tree representations are thus limited in that they cannot account for these phenomena. Although DOP models for a number of richer representations have been explored (e.g. Tugwell 1995), these approaches have remained context-free in their generative power.

In this chapter, we show how a DOP model can be developed for representations that are beyond context-free. We will use the representations defined by Lexical-Functional Grammar theory (Kaplan & Bresnan 1982; Kaplan 1989), which consist of a surface constituent tree enriched with a corresponding functional structure, and provide a new instantiation for the four parameters of the DOP architecture. We will refer to the resulting model as "LFG-DOP".

1 A DOP model for Lexical-Functional representations

1.1 Representations
The representations defined by LFG theory (Kaplan & Bresnan 1982; Kaplan 1989) consist of a c-structure, an f-structure and a mapping ϕ between them. The c-structure is a tree that describes the surface constituent structure of an utterance; the f-structure is an attribute-value matrix marking the grammatical relations of subject, predicate and object, as well as providing agreement features and semantic forms; and ϕ is a correspondence function that maps nodes of the c-structure into

126

units of the f-structure. The following figure shows a representation for the utterance *Kim eats*. (We leave out some features to keep the example simple.)

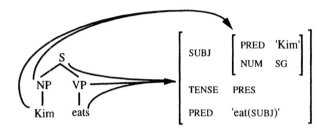

Figure 10.1. A representation for *Kim eats*

Note that the φ correspondence function gives an explicit character-ization of the relation between the superficial and underlying syntactic properties of an utterance, indicating how certain parts of the string carry information about particular units of underlying structure. As such, it will play a crucial role in our definition for the fragments of LFG-DOP. In figure 10.1 we see for instance that the NP node maps to the subject f-structure, and the S and VP nodes map to the outermost f-structure.

It is generally the case that the nodes in a subtree carry information only about the f-structure units that the subtree's root gives access to. The notion of accessibility is made precise in the following definition:

An f-structure unit f is φ-*accessible* from a node n iff either n is φ-linked to f (that is, $f = φ(n)$) or f is contained within $φ(n)$ (that is, there is a chain of attributes that leads from $φ(n)$ to f).

All the f-structure units in figure 10.1 are φ-accessible from for instance the S node and the VP node, but the TENSE and top-level PRED are not φ-accessible from the NP node.

According to the LFG representation theory, c-structures and f-structures must satisfy certain formal well-formedness conditions. A c-structure/f-structure pair is a *valid* LFG representation only if it satisfies the Nonbranching Dominance, Uniqueness, Coherence and Completeness conditions (Kaplan & Bresnan 1982). Nonbranching Dominance demands that no c-structure category appears twice in a nonbranching dominance chain; Uniqueness asserts that there can be at most one value for any attribute in the f-structure; Coherence prohibits the appearance of grammatical functions that are not governed by the lexical predicate; and Completeness requires that all the functions that a predicate governs appear as attributes in the local f-structure.

1.2 Fragments

Many different DOP models are compatible with the system of LFG representations. Following Bod & Kaplan (1998b), we give a relatively straightforward extension of DOP1 where the fragments are extended to take correspondences and f-structure features into account. That is, the fragments for LFG-DOP consist of connected subtrees whose nodes are in φ-correspondence with the correponding sub-units of f-structures. To give a precise definition of LFG-DOP fragments, it is convenient to redefine the fragments of DOP1 in terms of fragment-producing operations, also called "decomposition operations". (We already used the notion of decomposition in a more informal fashion in chapter 8.)

The fragments of DOP1 can be defined by the following two decomposition operations:

(1) *Root*: the *Root* operation selects any node of a tree to be the root of the new subtree and erases all nodes except the selected node and the nodes it dominates.

(2) *Frontier*: the *Frontier* operation then chooses a set (possibly empty) of nodes in the new subtree different from its root and erases all subtrees dominated by the chosen nodes.

Notice that *Root* and *Frontier* define exactly the same bag of subtrees as definitions (1)-(3) in section 2 of chapter 2. We now extend *Root* and *Frontier* so that they also apply to the nodes of the c-structure in LFG, while respecting the fundamental principles of c-structure/f-structure correspondence.

When a node is selected by the *Root* operation, all nodes outside of that node's subtree are erased, just as in DOP1. Further, for LFG-DOP, all φ links leaving the erased nodes are removed and all f-structure units that are not φ-accessible from the remaining nodes are erased. *Root* thus maintains the intuitive correlation between nodes and the information in their corresponding f-structures. For example, if *Root* selects the NP in figure 10.1, then the f-structure corresponding to the S node is erased, giving 10.2 as a possible fragment:

Figure 10.2. An LFG-DOP fragment obtained by the *Root* operation

In addition the *Root* operation deletes from the remaining f-structure all semantic forms that are local to f-structures that correspond to erased c-structure nodes, and it thereby also maintains the fundamental two-way connection between words and meanings. Thus, if *Root* selects the VP node so that the NP is erased, the subject semantic form "Kim" is also deleted:

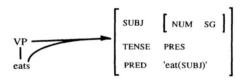

Figure 10.3. Another LFG-DOP fragment

As with DOP1, the *Frontier* operation then selects a set of frontier nodes and deletes all subtrees they dominate. Like *Root*, it also removes the φ links of the deleted nodes and erases any semantic form that corresponds to any of those nodes. *Frontier* does not delete any other f-structure features, however. This reflects the fact that all features are φ-accessible from the fragment's root even when nodes below the frontier are erased. For instance, if the VP in 10.1 is selected as a frontier node, *Frontier* erases the predicate 'eat(SUBJ)' from the fragment:

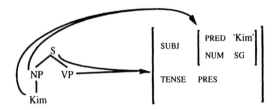

Figure 10.4. An LFG-DOP fragment obtained by the *Frontier* operation

Note that the *Root* and *Frontier* operations retain the subject's NUM feature in the VP-rooted fragment in figure 10.3, even though the subject NP is not present. This reflects the fact, usually encoded in particular grammar rules or lexical entries, that verbs of English carry agreement features for their subjects. On the other hand, the fragment in 10.4 retains the predicate's TENSE feature, reflecting the possibility that English subjects might also carry information about their predicate's tense. Subject-tense agreement as encoded in 10.4 is a pattern seen in some languages (e.g. the split-ergativity pattern of languages like Hindi, Urdu and Georgian) and thus there is no universal principle by which fragments such as in 10.4 can be ruled out. But in order to represent directly the possibility that subject-tense agreement is not a dependency of English, we also allow an S-fragment in which the TENSE feature is deleted, as in 10.5.

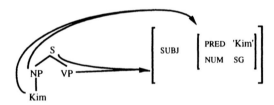

Figure 10.5. An LFG-DOP fragment obtained by the *Discard* operation

The fragment in 10.5 is produced by a third decomposition operation, *Discard*, defined to construct generalizations of the fragments supplied by *Root* and *Frontier*. *Discard* acts to delete combinations of attribute-value pairs subject to the following condition: *Discard* does not delete pairs whose values φ-correspond to remaining c-structure nodes.

This condition maintains the essential correspondences of LFG representations: if a c-structure and an f-structure are paired in one fragment by *Root* and *Frontier*, then *Discard* also pairs that c-structure with all generalizations of that fragment's f-structure. The fragment in 10.5 results from applying *Discard* to the TENSE feature in 10.4. *Discard* also produces fragments such as in 10.6, where the subject's number in 10.3 has been deleted:

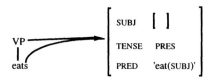

Figure 10.6. Another LFG-DOP fragment obtained by *Discard*

Again, since we have no language-specific knowledge apart from the corpus, we have no basis for ruling out fragments like in figure 10.6. Indeed, it is quite intuitive to omit the subject's number in fragments derived from sentences with past-tense verbs or modals. Thus the specification of *Discard* reflects the fact that LFG representations, unlike LFG grammars, do not indicate unambiguously the c-structure source (or sources) of their f-structure feature values.

1.3 The composition operation

In LFG-DOP the operation for combining fragments, again indicated by ∘, is carried out in two steps. First the c-structures are combined by left-most substitution subject to the category-matching condition, just as in DOP1. This is followed by the recursive unification of the f-structures corresponding to the matching nodes. The result retains the φ correspondences of the fragments being combined. A derivation for an LFG-DOP representation R is a sequence of fragments the first of which is labeled with S and for which the iterative application of the composition operation produces R.

We illustrate the two-stage composition operation by means of a few simple examples. We therefore assume a corpus containing the representation in figure 10.1 for the sentence *Kim eats* and the representation in 10.7 for the sentence *People ate*.

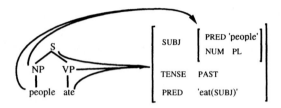

Figure 10.7. Corpus representation for *People ate*

Figure 10.8 shows the effect of the LFG-DOP composition operation using two fragments from this corpus. The VP-rooted fragment is substituted for the VP in the first fragment, and the second f-structure unifies with the first f-structure, resulting into a representation for the new sentence *Kim ate*.

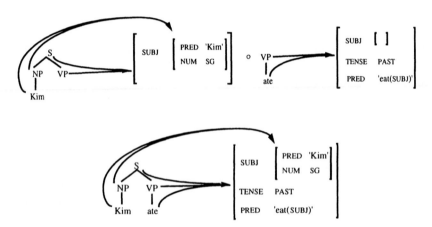

Figure 10.8. Illustration of the LFG-DOP composition operation yielding a representation for *Kim ate*

This representation satisfies the well-formedness conditions and is therefore valid. Note that in LFG-DOP, as in the tree-based DOP models, the same representation may be produced by several distinct derivations involving different fragments.

Another valid representation for the sentence *Kim ate* could be composed from a fragment for *Kim* that does not preserve the number feature:

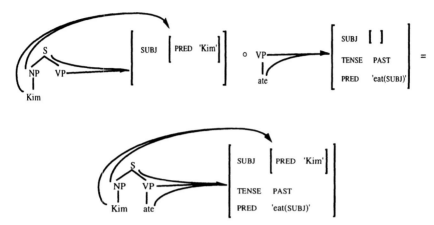

Figure 10.9. Another representation for *Kim ate* with unmarked number

Contrary to intuition, the subject in this representation is not marked for number. While there is no representational reason to exclude the result in figure 10.9 in favor of the one in 10.8, the probability models we discuss below have the desirable property that they tend to assign higher probabilities to more specific representations containing fewest feature generalizations, such as in 10.8.

The following derivation produces a valid representation for the intuitively ungrammatical sentence *People eats*:

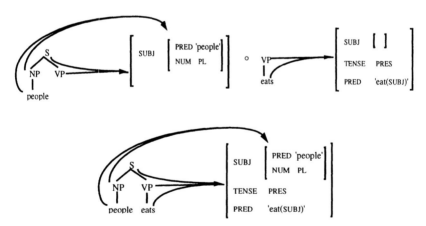

Figure 10.10. A valid representation for the ungrammatical sentence
People eats

This system of fragments and composition thus provides a representational basis for a robust model of language comprehension in that it assigns at least some representations to many strings that would generally be regarded as ill-formed. A correlate of this advantage, however, is the fact it does not offer a direct formal account of metalinguistic judgments of grammaticality. Nevertheless, we can reconstruct the notion of grammaticality by means of the following definition:

> A sentence is *grammatical with respect to a corpus* if and only if it has at least one valid representation with at least one derivation whose fragments are produced only by *Root* and *Frontier* and not by *Discard*.

Thus the system is robust in that it assigns three representations (singular, plural, and unmarked as the subject's number) to the string *People eats*, based on fragments for which the number feature of *people*, *eats*, or both has been discarded. But unless the corpus contains non-plural instances of *people* or non-singular instances of *eats*, there will be no *Discard*-free derivation and the string will be classified as ungrammatical (with respect to the corpus).

1.4 Probability models

As in tree-based DOP models, an LFG-DOP representation R can typically be derived in many different ways. If each derivation D has a probability $P(D)$, then the probability of deriving R is again the probability of producing it by any of its derivations. This is the sum of the individual derivation probabilities, as shown in (1):

(1) $P(R) = \Sigma_{D \text{ derives } R} P(D)$

An LFG-DOP derivation is also produced by a stochastic process. It starts by randomly choosing a fragment whose c-structure is labeled with the initial category (e.g. S). At each subsequent step, a next fragment is chosen at random from among the fragments that can be composed with the current subanalysis. The chosen fragment is composed with the current subanalysis to produce a new one; the process stops when an analysis results with no nonterminal leaves. We will call the set of composable fragments at a certain step in the stochastic process the *competition set* at that step. Let CP(f | CS) denote the probability of choosing a fragment f from a competition set CS containing f, then the probability of a derivation $D = \langle f_1, f_2 \dots f_k \rangle$ is

$$(2) \qquad P(\langle f_1, f_2 \dots f_k \rangle) = \prod_i CP(f_i \mid CS_i)$$

where the *competition probability* CP(f | CS) is expressed in terms of fragment probabilities P(f) by the formula

$$(3) \qquad CP(f \mid CS) = \frac{P(f)}{\sum_{f \in CS} P(f')}$$

The fragment probabilities P(f) can be computed by the relative frequencies of the fragments in the corpus.[14]

  DOP1 is the special case where there are no conditions of validity other than the ones that are enforced at each step of the stochastic process by the composition operation. This is not generally the case and is certainly not the case for the Completeness Condition of LFG representations: Completeness is a property of a final representation that cannot be evaluated at any intermediate steps of the process. However, we can define probabilities for the valid representations by sampling only from such representations in the output of the stochastic process. The probability of sampling a particular valid representation R is given by

$$(4) \qquad P(R \mid R \text{ is valid}) = \frac{P(R)}{\sum_{R' \text{ is valid}} P(R')}$$

This formula assigns probabilities to valid representations whether or not the stochastic process guarantees validity. The valid represensions for a particular word string W are obtained by a further sampling step and their probabilities are given by:

$$(5) \qquad P(R \mid R \text{ is valid and yields } W) = \frac{P(R)}{\sum_{R' \text{ is valid and yields } W} P(R')}$$

---

[14] There may be several other ways to compute fragment probabilities, for instance by random field induction as proposed in Cormons (forthcoming).

The formulas (1) through (5) will be part of any LFG-DOP probability model. The models will differ only in how the competition sets are defined, and this in turn depends on which well-formedness conditions are enforced on-line during the stochastic branching process and which are evaluated by the off-line validity sampling process.

One model, which we call M1, is a straightforward extension of DOP1's probability model. This computes the competition sets only on the basis of the category-matching condition, leaving all other well-formedness conditions for off-line sampling. Thus for M1 the competition sets are defined simply in terms of the categories of a fragment's c-structure root node. Suppose that $F_{i-1} = f_1 \circ f_2 \circ ... \circ f_{i-1}$ is the current subanalysis at the beginning of step i in the process, that $LNC(F_{i-1})$ denotes the category of the leftmost nonterminal node of the c-structure of F_{i-1}, and that $r(f)$ is interpreted as the root node category of f's c-structure component. Then the competition set for the ith step is

(6) $CS_i = \{ f : r(f)=LNC(F_{i-1}) \}$

Since these competition sets depend only on the category of the leftmost nonterminal of the current c-structure, the competition sets group together all fragments with the same root category, independent of any other properties they may have or that a particular derivation may have. The competition probability for a fragment can be expressed by the formula

(7) $CP(f) = \dfrac{P(f)}{\sum_{f' \in \{f'': r(f'') = r(f)\}} P(f')}$

We see that the choice of a fragment at a particular step in the stochastic process depends only on the category of its root node; other well-formedness properties of the representation are not used in making fragment selections. Thus, with this model the stochastic process may produce many invalid representations; we rely on sampling of valid representations and the conditional probabilities given by (4) and (5) to take the Uniqueness, Coherence, and Completeness Conditions into account.

Another possible model (M2) defines the competition sets so that they take a second condition, Uniqueness, into account in addition to the root node category. For M2 the competing fragments at a particular step in the stochastic derivation process are those whose c-structures have the same root node category as $\text{LNC}(F_{i-1})$ and also whose f-structures are consistently unifiable with the f-structure of F_{i-1}. Thus the competition set for the ith step is

(8) CS_i =
        $\{ f : r(f){=}\text{LNC}(F_{i-1})$ and f is unifiable with the f-structure of $F_{i-1} \}$

Although it is still the case that the category-matching condition is independent of the derivation, the unifiability requirement means that the competition sets vary according to the representation produced by the sequence of previous steps in the stochastic process. Unifiability must be determined at each step in the process to produce a new competition set, and the competition probability remains dependent on the particular step:

(9) $$\text{CP}(f_i \mid \text{CS}_i) = \frac{P(f_i)}{\sum_{f \in \{f: r(f)=r(f_i) \text{ and } f \text{ is unifiable with } F_{i-1}\}} P(f')}$$

On this model we again rely on sampling and the conditional probabilities (4) and (5) to take just the Coherence and Completeness Conditions into account.

In model M3 we define the stochastic process to enforce three conditions, Coherence, Uniqueness and category-matching, so that it only produces representations with well-formed c-structures that correspond to coherent and consistent f-structures. The competition probabilities for this model are given by the obvious extension of (9). It is not possible, however, to construct a model in which the Completeness Condition is enforced during the derivation process. This is because the satisfiability of the Completeness Condition depends not only on the results of previous steps of a derivation but also on the following steps (see Kaplan & Bresnan 1982). This nonmonotonic property means that the appropriate step-wise competition sets cannot be defined and that this condition can only be enforced at the final stage of validity sampling.

In each of these three models the category-matching condition is evaluated on-line during the derivation process while other conditions are either evaluated on-line or off-line by the after-the-fact sampling process. LFG-DOP is crucially different from the tree-based DOP models in that at least one validity requirement, the Completeness Condition, must always be left to the post-derivation process. Note that a number of other models are possible which enforce other combinations of these three conditions.

2 Illustration and properties of LFG-DOP

We illustrate LFG-DOP using a very small corpus consisting of the two simplified LFG representations shown in figure 10.11.

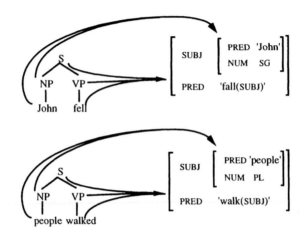

Figure 10.11. An example corpus of two simplified LFG representations

The fragments from this corpus can be composed to provide represen-tations for the two observed sentences plus two new utterances, *John walked* and *People fell*. This is sufficient to demonstrate that the probability models M1 and M2 assign different probabilities to particular representations. We have omitted the TENSE feature and the lexical categories N and V to reduce the number of the fragments we have to deal with. Applying the *Root* and *Frontier* operators systematically to the representation for *John fell* produces the fragments in the first column of figure 10.12, while the second column shows the additional f-structure that is associated with each c-structure by the *Discard* operation.

A total of 12 fragments are produced from this representation, and by analogy 12 fragments with either PL or unmarked NUM values will also result from *People walked*. Note that the [S NP VP] fragment with the unspecified NUM value is produced for both sentences and thus its corpus frequency is 2. There are 14 other S-rooted fragments, 4 NP-rooted fragments, and 4 VP-rooted fragments; each of these occurs only once.

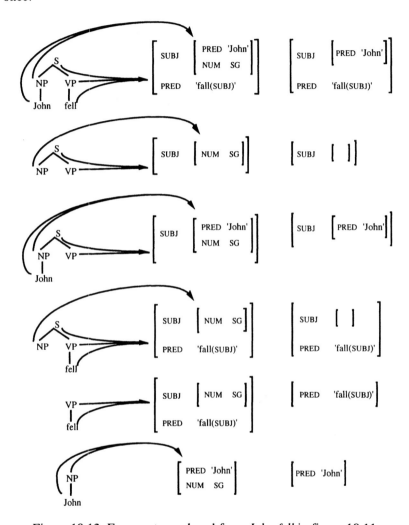

Figure 10.12. Fragments produced from *John fell* in figure 10.11.

These fragments can be used to derive three different representations for *John walked* (singular, plural, and unmarked as the subject's number). To facilitate the presentation of our derivations and probability calculations, we denote each fragment by an abbreviated name that indicates its c-structure root-node category, the sequence of its frontier-node labels, and whether its subject's number is SG, PL, or unmarked (indicated by U). Thus the first fragment in figure 10.12 is referred to as S/John-fell/SG and the unmarked fragment that *Discard* produces from it is referred to as S/John-fell/U. Given this naming convention, we can specify one of the derivations for *John walked* by the expression S/NP-VP/U ∘ NP/John/SG ∘ VP/walked/U, corresponding to an analysis in which the subject's number is marked as SG. The fragment VP/walked/U of course comes from *People walked*, the second corpus sentence, and does not appear in figure 10.12.

Model M1 evaluates only the root-category condition during the stochastic branching process, and the competition sets are fixed independent of the derivation. The probability of choosing the fragment S/NP-VP/U, given that an S-rooted fragment is required, is always 2/16, its frequency divided by the sum of the frequencies of all the S fragments. Similarly, the probability of then choosing NP/John/SG to substitute at the NP frontier node is 1/4, since the NP competition set contains 4 fragments each with frequency 1. Thus, under model M1 the probability of producing the complete derivation S/NP-VP/U ∘ NP/John/SG ∘ VP/walked/U is 2/16×1/4×1/4=2/256. This probability is small because it indicates the likelihood of this derivation compared to other derivations for *John walked* and for the three other analyzable strings. The computation of the other M1 derivation probabilities for *John walked* is left to the reader. There are 5 different derivations for the representation with SG number and 5 for the PL number, while there are only 3 ways of producing the unmarked number U. The conditional probabilities for the particular representations (SG, PL, U) can be calculated by formulas (1) and (5), and are given below.

$$P(\text{NUM=SG} \mid \text{valid and yield} = \textit{John walked}) = \quad .353$$
$$P(\text{NUM=PL} \mid \text{valid and yield} = \textit{John walked}) = \quad .353$$
$$P(\text{NUM=U} \mid \text{valid and yield} = \textit{John walked}) = \quad .294$$

We see that the two specific representations are equally likely and each of them is more probable than the representation with unmarked NUM.

Model M2 produces a slightly different distribution of probabilities. Under this model, the consistency requirement is used in addition to the root-category matching requirement to define the competition sets at each step of the branching process. This means that the first fragment that instantiates the NUM feature to either SG or PL constrains the competition sets for the following choices in a derivation. Thus, having chosen the NP/John/SG fragment in the derivation S/NP-VP/U ∘ NP/John/SG ∘ VP/walked/U, only 3 VP fragments instead of 4 remain in the competition set at the next step, since the VP/walked/PL fragment is no longer available. The probability for this derivation under model M2 is therefore $2/16 \times 1/4 \times 1/3 = 2/192$, slightly higher than the probability assigned to it by M1. Table 10.1 shows the complete set of derivations and their M2 probabilities for *John walked*.

S/NP-VP/U ∘ NP/John/SG ∘ VP/walked/U	SG	2/16 x 1/4 x 1/3
S/NP-VP/SG ∘ NP/John/SG ∘ VP/walked/U	SG	1/16 x 1/3 x 1/3
S/NP-VP/SG ∘ NP/John/U ∘ VP/walked/U	SG	1/16 x 1/3 x 1/3
S/NP-walked/U ∘ NP/John/SG	SG	1/16 x 1/4
S/John-VP/SG ∘ VP/walked/U	SG	1/16 x 1/3

P(NUM=SG and yield = *John walked*) = 35/576 = .061

P(NUM=SG | valid and yield = *John walked*) = 70/182 = .38

S/NP-VP/U ∘ NP/John/U ∘ VP/walked/PL	PL	2/16 x 1/4 x 1/4
S/NP-VP/PL ∘ NP/John/U ∘ VP/walked/PL	PL	1/16 x 1/3 x 1/3
S/NP-VP/PL ∘ NP/John/U ∘ VP/walked/U	PL	1/16 x 1/3 x 1/3
S/NP-walked/PL ∘ NP/John/U	PL	1/16 x 1/3
S/John-VP/U ∘ VP/walked/PL	PL	1/16 x 1/4

P(NUM=PL and yield = *John walked*) = 33.5/576 = .058

P(NUM=PL | valid and yield = *John walked*) = 67/182 = .37

S/NP-VP/U ∘ NP/John/U ∘ VP/walked/U	U	2/16 x 1/4 x 1/4
S/NP-walked/U ∘ NP/John/U	U	1/16 x 1/4
S/John-VP/U ∘ VP/walked/U	U	1/16 x 1/4

P(NUM=U and yield = *John walked*) = 22.5/576 = .039

P(NUM=U | valid and yield = *John walked*) = 45/182 = .25

Table 10.1: Model M2 derivations, subject number features, and probabilities for *John walked*

The total probability for the derivations that produce *John walked* is .158, and the conditional probabilities for the three representations are:

$P(NUM=SG \mid valid \ and \ yield = John \ walked) = \quad .38$

$P(NUM=PL \mid valid \ and \ yield = John \ walked) = \quad .37$

$P(NUM=U \mid valid \ and \ yield = John \ walked) = \quad .25$

For model M2 the unmarked representation is less likely than under M1, and now there is a slight bias in favor of the value SG over PL. The SG value is favored because it is carried by substitutions for the left-most word of the utterance and thus reduces competition for subsequent choices. The value PL would be more probable for the sentence *People fell*. Thus both probability models give higher probability to the more specific representations. Moreover, M1 assigns the same probability to SG and PL, whereas M2 doesn't. M2 reflects a left-to-right bias (which might be psycholinguistically interesting -- a so-called primacy effect), whereas M1 is, like DOP1, order independent.

It turns out that all three LFG-DOP probability models (M1, M2 and M3) display a preference for the most specific representation. This preference partly depends on the number of derivations: specific representations tend to have more derivations than generalized (i.e., unmarked) representations, and consequently tend to get higher probabilities -- other things being equal. However, this preference also depends on the number of feature values: the more feature values, the longer the minimal derivation length must be in order to get a preference for the most specific representation (Cormons, forthcoming).

The bias in favor of more specific representations, and consequently fewer *Discard*-produced feature generalizations, is especially interesting for the interpretation of ill-formed input strings. Bod & Kaplan (1997) show that in analyzing an intuitively ungrammatical string like *These boys walks*, there is a probabilistic accumulation of evidence for the plural interpretation over the singular and unmarked one (for all models M1, M2 and M3). This is because both *These* and *boys* carry the PL feature while only *walks* is a source for the SG feature, leading to more derivations for the PL reading of *These boys walks*. In case of "equal evidence" as in the ill-formed string *Boys walks*, model M1 assigns the same probability to PL and SG, while models M2 and M3 prefer the PL interpretation due to their left-to-right bias.

The DOP model we presented in this chapter is significant in that previous DOP models were based on context-free tree representations which cannot adequately represent all linguistic phenomena. We showed that a DOP model for LFG representations triggers a new, corpus-based notion of grammaticality and that its probability models display a preference for the most specific analysis containing the fewest number of feature generalizations, which is especially interesting with respect to the interpretation of ill-formed strings.

As to the computational aspects of LFG-DOP, the problem of finding the most probable representation of a sentence is NP-hard even for DOP1 (chapter 4). This problem may be tackled by Monte Carlo sampling techniques or by computing the Viterbi n best derivations of a sentence. Other optimization heuristics may consist of restricting the fragment space, for example by putting an upper bound on the fragment depth, or by constraining the decomposition operations. To date, a couple of LFG-DOP implementations are either operational (Cormons, forthcoming) or under development, and corpora with LFG representations have recently been developed (at XRCE, France and Xerox PARC, California). These corpora will be used to test whether our working hypothesis can also be confirmed for non-context-free representations.

Conclusion: linguistics revisited

We have designed an experience-based theory of language which learns how to provide appropriate linguistic representations for an unlimited set of utterances by generalizing from examples of representations of previously occurring utterances. This probabilistic theory operates by decomposing the given representations into fragments and recomposing those pieces to analyze new utterances.

We have shown how our theory compares with other probabilistic language models (chapter 3), how it can be implemented (chapter 4) and tested (chapter 5), how it can learn new words and structures (chapters 6 and 7), how it can be used for semantic interpretation (chapter 8) and spoken dialogue processing (chapter 9), how recency and discourse structure can be brought into the picture (chapter 8), and how experience-based models for non-context-free representations can be developed (chapter 10). The probability models we designed display a number of important properties, among which are a preference for representations which can be constructed out of the largest possible fragments (and thus for representations that are most similar to previously seen utterance-representations), a preference for representations which generalize over a minimal number of features (in case of ill-formed input), and a preference for representations which contain a minimal number of mismatches (in case of unknown input).

We will not sum up all the findings that have been presented in this book. Rather we emphasize the most important outcome, namely that any systematic restriction of the fragments seems to jeopardize the statistical dependencies that are needed for predicting the appropriate structure of a sentence. We derive from this that the productive units of natural language cannot be defined in terms of a minimal set of rules (or constraints or principles), as is usually attempted in linguistic theory, but need to be defined in terms of a large, redundant set of previously experienced structures with virtually no restriction on size and complexity.

If this outcome is generally true, it has important consequences for linguistic theory. It means that the knowledge of a speaker/hearer cannot be understood as a grammar, but as a statistical ensemble of language experiences that changes slightly every time a new utterance is perceived or produced. The regularities we observe in language may be viewed as emergent phenomena, but they cannot be summarized into a consistent non-redundant system that unequivocally defines the structures of new utterances. The notion of "Universal Grammar" becomes obsolete, and should be substituted by the notion of "Universal Representation" for language experiences. In this perspective, the role for linguistic theory would be to discover this Universal Representation formalism (which should apply to all linguistic phenomena and all natural languages), together with the operations that language users apply on representations to produce representations for new utterances. The problem of language acquisition would be the problem of acquiring examples of representations from linguistic experiences guided by the Universal Representation formalism. Language change could be explained as a side-effect of updating the statistical ensemble of language experiences. And if there is anything in the human language faculty that is "innate", then it should be (1) the Universal Representation for linguistic experiences, and (2) the capacity to take apart and recombine these experiences.

References

Aha, D., D. Kibler and M. Albert, 1991. "Instance-Based Learning Algorithms", *Machine Learning* 6, 37-66.

Alshawi, H. 1994. "Qualitative and Quantitative Models of Speech Translation", *The Balancing Act, Combining Symbolic and Statistical Approaches to Language, Proceedings of the Workshop*, ACL, New Mexico State University.

Aust, H., M. Oerder, F. Seide and V. Steinbiss, 1995. "The Philips automatic train timetable information system", *Speech Communication*, 17, 249-262.

Balcazar, J., J. Diaz and J. Gabarro, 1988. *Structural Complexity*, Springer Verlag, Berlin.

Berg, M. van den, R. Bod and R. Scha, 1994. "A Corpus-Based Approach to Semantic Interpretation", *Proceedings Ninth Amsterdam Colloquium*, Amsterdam, The Netherlands.

Black, E., S. Abney, D. Flickenger, C. Gnadiec, R. Grishman, P. Harrison, D. Hindle, R. Ingria, F. Jelinek, J. Klavans, M. Liberman, M. Marcus, S. Roukos, B. Santorini and T. Strzalkowski, 1991. "A Procedure for Quantitatively Comparing the Syntactic Coverage of English", *Proceedings DARPA Speech and Natural Language Workshop*, Pacific Grove, Morgan Kaufmann.

Black, E., J. Lafferty and S. Roukos, 1992. "Development and Evaluation of a Broad-Coverage Probabilistic Grammar of English-Language Computer Manuals", *Proceedings ACL'92*, Newark, Delaware.

Black, E., R. Garside and G. Leech, 1993a. *Statistically-Driven Computer Grammars of English: The IBM/Lancaster Approach*, Rodopi: Amsterdam-Atlanta.

146

Black, E., F. Jelinek, J. Lafferty, D. Magerman, R. Mercer and S. Roukos, 1993b. "Towards History-Based Grammars: Using Richer Models for Probabilistic Parsing", *Proceedings ACL'93*, Columbus, Ohio.

Bock, J. 1986. "Syntactic persistence in language production", *Cognitive Psychology*, 18, 355-387.

Bod, R. 1991. "Data Oriented Parsing", *Proceedings Computational Linguistics in the Netherlands 1991*, Amsterdam, The Netherlands.

Bod, R. 1992. "A Computational Model of Language Performance: Data Oriented Parsing", *Proceedings COLING-92*, Nantes, France.

Bod, R. 1993a. "Using an Annotated Corpus as a Stochastic Grammar", *Proceedings European Chapter of the ACL'93*, Utrecht, The Netherlands.

Bod, R. 1993b. "Monte Carlo Parsing", *Proceedings Third International Workshop on Parsing Technologies*, Tilburg/Durbuy, The Netherlands/ Belgium.

Bod, R. 1993c. "Data Oriented Parsing as a General Framework for Stochastic Language Processing", in: K. Sikkel and A. Nijholt (eds.), *Parsing Natural Language*, TWLT6, Twente University, The Netherlands.

Bod, R. 1993d. "Using an Annotated Language Corpus as a Virtual Stochastic Grammar", *Proceedings AAAI-93*, Menlo Park, Ca.

Bod, R. 1995a. "The Problem of Computing the Most Probable Tree in Data-Oriented Parsing and Stochastic Tree Grammars", *Proceedings European chapter of the ACL'95*, Dublin, Ireland.

Bod, R. 1995b. *Enriching Linguistics with Statistics: Performance Models of Natural Language*, ILLC Dissertation Series 1995-14, University of Amsterdam, The Netherlands.

Bod, R. 1996a. "Efficient Algorithms for Parsing the DOP Model? A Reply to Joshua Goodman". *Computational Linguistics Archive cmp-lg/9605031*. (available from http://xxx.lanl.gov/cmp-lg/9605031)

Bod, R. 1996b. "Two Questions about Data-Oriented Parsing", *Proceedings Fourth Workshop on Very Large Corpora*, COLING-96, Copenhagen, Denmark.

Bod, R. 1996c. "Monte Carlo Parsing", in H. Bunt and M. Tomita (eds.) *Recent Advances in Parsing Technology*, Kluwer Academic Publishers. 255-280.

Bod, R. 1998. "Spoken Dialogue Interpretation with the DOP Model", *Proceedings COLING-ACL'98*, Montreal, Canada.

Bod, R. and R. Scha, 1994. "Prediction and Disambiguation by means of Data-Oriented Parsing", *Proceedings Twente Workshop on Language Technology (TWLT8)*, Twente, The Netherlands.

Bod, R., R. Bonnema and R. Scha, 1996. "A Data-Oriented Approach to Semantic Interpretation", *Proceedings Workshop on Corpus-Oriented Semantic Analysis*, ECAI-96, Budapest, Hungary.

Bod, R. and R. Scha, 1996. "Data-Oriented Language Processing. An Overview." *Technical Report LP-96-13*, Institute for Logic, Language and Computation, University of Amsterdam, The Netherlands.

Bod, R., R. Bonnema and R. Scha, 1997. "Data-Oriented Semantic Interpretation", *Proceedings Second International Workshop on Computational Semantics*, IWCS-II, Tilburg, The Netherlands.

Bod, R. and R. Kaplan 1997. "On Performance models for Lexical-Functional Analysis", Paper presented at the *Computational Psycholinguistics Conference* 1997, Berkeley (Ca).

Bod, R. and R. Scha, 1997. Data-Oriented Language Processing. In S. Young and G. Bloothooft (eds.) *Corpus-Based Methods in Language and Speech Processing*, Kluwer Academic Publishers, Boston. 137-173.

Bod, R. and R. Kaplan, 1998a. "Grammaticality, Robustness, and Specificity in a Probabilistic Approach to Lexical Functional Analysis", *Proceedings LFG Conference and Workshops*, Brisbane, Australia.

Bod, R. and R. Kaplan, 1998b. "A Probabilistic Corpus-Driven Model for Lexical-Functional Analysis", *Proceedings COLING-ACL'98*, Montreal, Canada.

Bonnema, R. 1996. *Data-Oriented Semantics*, Master's Thesis, Department of Computational Linguistics, University of Amsterdam, The Netherlands.

Bonnema, R., R. Bod and R. Scha, 1997. "A DOP Model for Semantic Interpretation", *Proceedings ACL/EACL-97*, Madrid, Spain.

Booth, T. 1969. "Probabilistic Representation of Formal Languages", *Tenth Annual IEEE Symposium on Switching and Automata Theory*.

Booth, T. and R. Thompson, 1973. "Applying Probability Measures to Abstract Languages", *IEEE Transactions on Computers*, C-22(5).

Boros, M., W. Eckert, F. Gallwitz, G. Görz, G. Hanrieder and H. Niemann, 1996. "Towards understanding spontaneous speech: word accuracy vs. concept accuracy." *Proceedings ICSLP'96*, Philadelphia, PA.

Bourigault, D. 1993. "An Endogeneous Corpus-Based Method for Structural Noun Phrase Disambiguation", *Proceedings European Chapter of the ACL'93*, Utrecht, The Netherlands.

Boves, L., J. Landsbergen, R. Scha and G. van Noord, 1996. *Projectplan NWO Priority Programme Language and Speech Technology*, NWO, The Hague.

Bresnan, J. (ed.) 1982. *The Mental Representation of Grammatical Relations*, The MIT Press, Cambridge, MA.

Brew, C. 1995. "Stochastic HPSG", *Proceedings European chapter of the ACL'95*, Dublin, Ireland.

Briscoe, T. and J. Carroll, 1993. "Generalized Probabilistic LR Parsing of Natural Language (Corpora) with Unification-Based Grammars", *Computational Linguistics* 19(1), 25-59.

Briscoe, T. 1994. "Prospects for Practical Parsing of Unrestricted Text: Robust Statistical Parsing Techniques", N. Oostdijk and P. de Haan (eds.), *Corpus-based Research into Language*, Rodopi, Amsterdam.

Brill, E. 1993. "Transformation-Based Error-Driven Parsing", *Proceedings Third International Workshop on Parsing Technologies*, Tilburg/Durbuy, The Netherlands/Belgium.

Carbonell, J. 1979. "Towards a Self-Extending Parser", *Proceedings ACL'79*.

Carroll, J. and T. Briscoe, 1992. "Probabilistic Normalization and Unpacking of Packed Parse Forests for Unification-based

Grammars", *Working Notes Probabilistic Approaches to Natural Language*, AAAI Fall Symposium Series, Cambridge, Ma.

Carroll, J. and D. Weir, 1997. "Encoding Frequency Information in Lexicalized Grammars", *Proceedings 5th International Workshop on Parsing Technologies*, MIT, Cambridge, Ma.

Chiang, T., Y. Lin and K. Su, 1995. "Robust Learning, Smoothing, and Parameter Tying on Syntactic Ambiguity Resolution", *Computational Linguistics* 21(3).

Charniak, E. 1993. *Statistical Language Learning*, Cambridge (Mass.), The MIT Press.

Charniak, E. 1996. "Tree-bank Grammars", *Proceedings AAAI-96*, Menlo Park.

Charniak, E. 1997a. "Statistical Techniques for Natural Language Parsing", *AI Magazine*.

Charniak, E. 1997b. "Statistical Parsing with a Context-Free Grammar and Word Statistics", *Proceedings AAAI-97*, Menlo Park.

Chomsky, N. 1965. *Aspects of the Theory of Syntax*, Cambridge (Mass.), The MIT Press.

Christiansen, M. and M. MacDonald, 1998. "Individual Differences in Sentence Comprehension: The Importance of Experience", *The 11th Annual CUNY Conference on Human Sentence Processing*, Rutgers University.

Church, K. 1988. "A Stochastic Parts Program and Noun Phrase Parser for Unrestricted Text", *Proceedings ANLP'88*, Austin, Texas.

Church, K. and R. Patil, 1983. *Coping with Syntactic Ambiguity or How to Put the Block in the Box on the Table*, MIT/LCS/TM-216.

Church, K. and W. Gale, 1991. "A comparison of the enhanced Good-Turing and deleted estimation methods for estimating probabilities of English bigrams", *Computer Speech and Language* 5, 19-54.

Church, K. and R. Mercer, 1993. "Introduction to the Special Issue on Computational Linguistics Using Large Corpora", *Computational Linguistics* 19(1), 1-24.

Cochran, W. 1963. *Sampling Techniques*, Wiley & Sons, New York (2nd edition).

Coleman, J. and J. Pierrehumbert, 1997. "Stochastic Phonological Grammars and Acceptability", *Proceedings Computational Phonology, Third Meeting of the ACL Special Interest Group in Computational Phonology*, Madrid, Spain.

Collins, M. 1996. "A new statistical parser based on bigram lexical dependencies", *Proceedings ACL'96*, Santa Cruz (Ca.).

Collins, M. 1997. "Three generative lexicalised models for statistical parsing", *Proceedings ACL'97*, Madrid, Spain.

Corazza, A., R. Gretter and G. Satta, 1991. "Stochastic Context-Free Grammars for Island-Driven Probabilistic Parsing", *Proceedings Second International Workshop on Parsing Technologies*, Cancun, Mexico.

Cormons, B. forthcoming. *Analyse et desambiguisation: Une approche purement à base de corpus (Data-Oriented Parsing) pour le formalisme des Grammaires Lexicales Fonctionnelles*, PhD thesis, Université de Rennes, France.

Deming, W. 1966. *Some Theory of Sampling*, Dover Publications, New York.

Eisner, J. 1996. "Three new probabilistic models for dependency parsing: an exploration", *Proceedings COLING-96*, Copenhagen, Denmark.

Eisner, J. 1997. "Bilexical Grammars and a Cubic-Time Probabilistic Parser", *Proceedings Fifth International Workshop on Parsing Technologies*, Boston, Mass.

Fenk-Oczlon, G. 1989. "Word frequency and word order in freezes", *Linguistics* 27, 517-556.

Fillmore, C., P. Kay and M. O'Connor, 1988. "Regularity and idiomaticity in grammatical constructions: the case of let alone", *Language* 64, 501-538.

Fu, K. 1974. "Syntactic methods in pattern recognition", *Mathematics in Science and Engineering, 112*, Academic Press.

Fu, K. 1982. *Syntactic Pattern Recognition and Applications*, Prentice-Hall.

Fujisaki, T. 1984. "An Approach to Stochastic Parsing", *Proceedings COLING-84*.

Fujisaki, T., F. Jelinek, J. Cocke, E. Black and T. Nishino, 1989. "A Probabilistic Method for Sentence Disambiguation", *Proceedings 1st Int. Workshop on Parsing Technologies*, Pittsburgh, PA.

Gale, W. and K. Church, 1994. "What is wrong with adding one?", N. Oostdijk and P. de Haan (eds.), *Corpus-based Research into Language*, Rodopi, Amsterdam.

Gale, W. and G. Sampson, 1995. "Good-Turing Frequency Estimation without Tears", *Journal of Quantitative Linguistics* 2(3), 217-237.

Gamut, L. T. F. 1991. *Logic, Language, and Meaning*, The University of Chicago Press.

Garside, R., G. Leech and G. Sampson, 1987. *The Computational Analysis of English: A Corpus-Based Approach*, Longman.

Gibson, E. 1990. "Recency preference and garden-path effects", *Proceedings of the 12th Cognitive Science Society*.

Gibson, E. and J. Loomis, 1994. "A Corpus Analysis of Recency Preference and Predicate Proximity", *Proceedings of the 16th Cognitive Science Society*, Lawrence Erlbaum, Hillsdale, NJ.

Good, I. 1953. "The Population Frequencies of Species and the Estimation of Population Parameters", *Biometrika* 40, 237-264.

Goodman, J. 1996. "Efficient Algorithms for Parsing the DOP Model", *Proceedings Empirical Methods in Natural Language Processing*, Philadelphia, PA.

Goodman, J. 1998. *Parsing Inside-Out*, Ph.D. thesis, Harvard University, Mass.

Graham, S., M. Harrison and W. Ruzzo, 1980. "An improved context-free recognizer", *ACM Transactions on Programming Languages and Systems*, 2(3), 415-462.

Grishman, R., C. Macleod and J. Sterling, 1992. "Evaluating Parsing Strategies Using Standardized Parse Files", *Proceedings ANLP'92*, Trento, Italy.

Halteren, H. van, and N. Oostdijk, 1988. "Using an Analyzed Corpus as a Linguistic Database", J. Roper (ed.) *Computers in Literary and Linguistic Computing*, Champion Slatkine, Paris, France.

Hammersley, J. and D. Handscomb, 1964. *Monte Carlo Methods*, Chapman and Hall, London.

Harmelen, F. van, and A. Bundy, 1988. "Explanation-Based Generalization = Partial Evaluation", *Artificial Intelligence* 36, 401-412.

Harrison, P., S. Abney, E. Black, D. Flickenger, C. Gnadiec, R. Grishman, D. Hindle, R. Ingria, M. Marcus, B. Santorini and T. Strzalkowski, 1991. "Evaluating Syntax Performance of Parser/Grammars", *Proceedings of the Natural Language Processing Systems Evaluation Workshop*, Berkeley, Ca.

Hasher, I. and W. Chromiak, 1977. "The processing of frequency information: an automatic mechanism?", *Journal of Verbal Learning and Verbal Behavior* 16, 173-184.

Hasher, I. and R. Zacks, 1984. "Automatic Processing of Fundamental Information: the case of frequency of occurrence", *American Psychologist* 39, 1372-1388.

Hemphill, C., J. Godfrey and G. Doddington, 1990. "The ATIS spoken language systems pilot corpus". *Proceedings DARPA Speech and Natural Language Workshop*, Hidden Valley, Morgan Kaufmann.

Hendriks, H. 1993. *Studied Flexibility, Categories and Types in Syntax and Semantics*, ILLC Dissertation Series 1993-5, University of Amsterdam, The Netherlands.

Hindle, D. and M. Rooth, 1993. "Structural Ambiguity and Lexical Relations", *Computational Linguistics*, 19(1), 103-120.

Hoeven, E. van der, 1995. *The Use of Data-Oriented Parsing as a Language Model for Speech Recognition*, Master's Thesis, Department of Computational Linguistics, University of Amsterdam, The Netherlands.

Jacoby, L. and L. Brooks, 1984. "Nonanalytic Cognition: Memory, Perception and Concept Learning", G. Bower (ed.), *Psychology of Learning and Motivation* (Vol. 18, 1-47), San Diego: Academic Press.

Jeffreys, H. 1948. *Theory of Probability*, Second Edition, Section 3.23, Oxford, Clarendon Press.

Jelinek, F. 1985. "The Development of an Experimental Discrete Dictation Recognizer", *IEEE'85* (Invited Paper).

Jelinek, F. and R. Mercer, 1985. "Probability Distribution Estimation from Sparse Data", *IBM Technical Disclosure Bulletin* 28, 2591-2594.

Jelinek, F., J. Lafferty and R. Mercer, 1990. *Basic Methods of Probabilistic Context Free Grammars*, Technical Report IBM RC 16374 (#72684), Yorktown Heights.

Johnson, M. 1996. "Ranking LFG Analyses", unpublished manuscript.

Johnson, W. 1932. Appendix (edited by R. Braithwaite) to "Probability Deductive and Inductive Problems", *Mind*, 41, 421-423.

Joshi, A. 1987. "Introduction to Tree-Adjoining Grammar", A. Manaster Ramer (ed.), *The Mathematics of Language*, J. Benjamins.

Joshi, A. and Y. Schabes, 1991. "Tree-Adjoining Grammars and Lexicalized Grammars", M. Nivat (ed.), *Definability and Recognizability of Sets of Trees*, Elsevier.

Joshi, A. and B. Srinivas, 1994. "Disambiguation of super parts of speech (or supertags): almost parsing", *Proceedings COLING-94*, Tokyo, Japan.

Joshi, A., K. Vijay-Shanker and D. Weir, 1991. "The Convergence of Mildly Context-Sensitive Grammar Formalisms", Sells et al. (eds.), *Foundational Issues in NLP*, MIT Press.

Juliano, C. and M. Tanenhaus, 1993. "Contingent Frequency Effects in Syntactic Ambiguity Resolution", *Fifteenth Annual Conference of the Cognitive Science Society*, 593-598, Hillsdale, NJ.

Jurafsky, D. 1996. "A probabilistic model of lexical and syntactic access and disambiguation", *Cognitive Science*, 20, 137-194.

Kaplan, R. 1989. "The Formal Architecture of Lexical-Functional Grammar", *Journal of Information Science and Engineering*, vol. 5, 305-322.

Kaplan, R. 1996. "A Probabilistic Approach to Lexical-Functional Analysis", *Proceedings of the 1996 LFG Conference and Workshops*, CSLI Publications, Stanford, Ca.

Kaplan, R. and J. Bresnan, 1982. "Lexical-Functional Grammar: A Formal System for Grammatical Representation", in J. Bresnan (ed.), *The Mental Representation of Grammatical Relations*, The MIT Press, Cambridge, Mass.

Karlsson, F., A. Voutilainen, J. Heikkila and A. Anttila, 1995. *Constraint Grammar, A Language-Independent System for Parsing Unrestricted Text*, Mouton de Gruyter: Berlin.

Katz, S. 1987. "Estimation of probabilities from sparse data for the language model component of a speech recognizer", *IEEE Transactions on Acoustics, Speech, and Signal Processing*, ASSP-35, 400-401.

Kausler, D. and J. Puckett, 1980. "Frequency Judgments and Correlated Cognitive Abilities in Young and Elderly Adults", *Journal of Gerontology* 35, 376-382.

Kay, M. 1980. *Algorithmic Schemata and Data Structures in Syntactic Processing*. Report CSL-80-12, Xerox PARC, Palo Alto, Ca.

Kempen, G. 1996. "Computational Models of Syntactic Processing in Human Language Comprehension", in A. Dijkstra and K. de Smedt (eds.), *Computational Psycholinguistics: Symbolic and subsymbolic models of language processing*. Taylor & Francis, London.

Kuiper, K. 1996. *Smooth Talkers*, Erlbaum, NJ.

Lafferty, J., D. Sleator and D. Temperley, 1992. "Grammatical Trigrams: a Probabilistic Model of Link Grammar", *Proceedings AAAI Fall Symposium on Probabilistic Approaches to Natural Language*, Cambridge, Mass.

Levelt, W. 1974. *Formal Grammars in Linguistics and Psycholinguistics (vol.I)*, Mouton, The Hague.

Liberman, M. 1991. "The Trend towards Statistical Models in Natural Language Processing", in E. Klein and F. Veltman (eds.), *Natural Language and Speech*, Springer Verlag, Berlin.

Liberman, M. and Y. Schabes, 1993. *Statistical Methods in Natural Language Processing*, Tutorial notes, EACL-93, Utrecht, The Netherlands.

Linz, P. 1990. *An Introduction to Formal Languages and Automata*. Heath & Co. Lexington, Mass.

MacDonald, M., N. Pearlmutter and M. Seidenberg, 1994. "Lexical Nature of Syntactic Ambiguity Resolution", *Psychological Review* 101, 676-703.

Magerman, D. and M. Marcus, 1991. "Pearl: A Probabilistic Chart Parser", *Proceedings EACL'91*, Berlin, Germany.

Magerman, D. and C. Weir, 1992. "Efficiency, Robustness and Accuracy in Picky Chart Parsing", *Proceedings ACL'92*, Newark, Delaware.

Magerman, D. 1993. "Expectation-Maximization for Data-Oriented Parsing", Technical Report IBM, Yorktown Heights, NY.

Magerman, D. 1995. "Statistical Decision-Tree Models for Parsing", *Proceedings ACL'95*, Cambridge, Mass.

Marcus, M., B. Santorini and M. Marcinkiewicz, 1993. "Building a Large Annotated Corpus of English: the Penn Treebank", *Computational Linguistics* 19(2).

Martin, W., K. Church and R. Patil, 1987. "Preliminary Analysis of a Breadth-first Parsing Algorithm: Theoretical and Experimental Results", in: L. Bolc (ed.), *Natural Language Parsing Systems*, Springer Verlag, Berlin.

Mehler, J. and P. Carey, 1968. "The interaction of veracity and syntax in the processing of sentences", *Perception and Psychophysics*, 3, 109-111.

Meyer, H. (ed.), 1956. *Symposium on Monte Carlo Methods*. Wiley, New York, NY.

Miller, S., D. Stallard, R. Bobrow and R. Schwarz, 1996. "A fully statistical approach to natural language interfaces", *Proceedings ACL'96*, Santa Cruz, Ca.

Mitchell, D., F. Cuetos and M. Corley, 1992. "Statistical versus Linguistic Determinants of Parsing Bias: Cross-linguistic Evidence", *Fifth Annual CUNY Conference on Human Sentence Processing*, New York, NY.

Motwani, R. and P. Raghavan, 1995. *Randomized Algorithms*, Cambridge University Press, Cambridge.

Nadas, A. 1985. "On Turing's formula for word probabilities", *IEEE Transactions on Acoustics, Speech, and Signal Processing*, ASSP-33, 1414-1416.

Nicol, J. and M. Pickering, 1993. "Processing Syntactically Ambiguous Sentences: Evidence from Semantic Priming", *Journal of Psycholinguistic Research*.

Noord, G. van, 1995. The intersection of finite state automata and definite clause grammars. *Proceedings ACL'95*, Boston.

Noord, G. van, G. Bouma, R. Koeling and M. Nederhof, 1997. *Robust Grammatical Analysis for Spoken Dialogue Systems*, unpublished manuscript.

Pearlmutter, N. and M. MacDonald, 1992. "Plausibility and Syntactic Ambiguity Resolution", *Proceedings 14th Annual Conf. of the Cognitive Society*.

Pereira, F. and Y. Schabes, 1992. "Inside-Outside Reestimation from Partially Bracketed Corpora", *Proceedings ACL'92*, Newark, Delaware.

Polanyi, L. and R. Scha, 1983. "On the Recursive Structure of Discourse", in K. Ehlich and H. van Riemsdijk (eds.), *Connectedness in Sentence, Discourse and Text*, pp141-178, Tilburg University, The Netherlands.

Polanyi, L. 1985. "A theory of discourse structure and discourse coherence", in *Proceedings of the 21st Regional Meeting of the Chicago Linguistics Society*. University of Chicago Press.

Price, P. 1994. "Combining Linguistic with Statistical Methods in Automatic Speech Understanding", *The Balancing Act, Combining Symbolic and Statistical Approaches to Language, Proceedings of the Workshop*, ACL, New Mexico State University, New Mexico.

Prince, A. and P. Smolensky, 1993. *Optimality theory: constraint interaction in generative grammar*, Technical Report of the Rutgers University Center for Cognitive Science.

Rajman, M. 1995a. *Apports d'une approche a base de corpus aux techniques de traitement automatique du langage naturel*, Ph.D. thesis, Ecole Nationale Superieure des Telecommunications, Paris, France.

Rajman, M. 1995b. "Approche Probabiliste de l'Analyse Syntaxique", *Traitement Automatique des Langues*, vol. 36(1-2).

Rajman, M. and J. Han, 1995. "Prise en compte de contraintes syntaxiques dans le cadre d'un système de reconnaissance de la parole", *Proceedings TALN'95*, Marseille, France.

Resnik, P. 1992. "Probabilistic Tree-Adjoining Grammar as a Framework for Statistical Natural Language Processing", *Proceedings COLING'92*, Nantes, France.

Rubin, D. and A. Wenzel, 1996. "One Hundred Years of Forgetting: A Quantitative Description of Retention", *Psychological Review*, vol. 103(4). 734-760.

Sampson, G. 1986. "A Stochastic Approach to Parsing", *Proceedings COLING'86*, Bonn, Germany.

Sampson, G. 1987. "Evidence against the 'Grammatical/Ungrammatical' Distinction", W. Meijs (ed.), *Corpus Linguistics and Beyond*, Rodopi, Amsterdam.

Sampson, G. 1995. *English for the Computer: The SUSANNE Corpus and Analytic Scheme*. Clarendon Press, Oxford.

Samuelsson, C. 1996. "Relating Turing's Formula and Zipf's Law", *Proceedings Fourth Workshop on Very Large Corpora*, COLING-96, Copenhagen, Denmark.

Santorini, B. 1990. *Part-of-Speech Tagging Guidelines for the Penn Treebank Project*, Dept. of Computer and Information Science, University of Pennsylvania, PA.

Santorini, B. 1991. *Bracketing Guidelines for the Penn Treebank Project*, Dept. of Computer and Information Science, University of Pennsylvania, PA.

Scha, R. 1990. "Taaltheorie en Taaltechnologie; Competence en Performance", in Q.A.M. de Kort and G.L.J. Leerdam (eds.), *Computertoepassingen in de Neerlandistiek*, Almere: Landelijke Vereniging van Neerlandici (LVVN-jaarboek).

Scha, R. 1992. "Virtuele Grammatica's en Creatieve Algoritmen", *Gramma/TTT* 1(1).

Scha, R. and L. Polanyi, 1988. "An Augmented Context-free Grammar for Discourse", *Proceedings COLING'88*, Budapest, Hungary.

Schaaf, B. 1998. *Metrical Structure in DOP*, Master's thesis, Department of Computational Linguistics, University of Amsterdam, The Netherlands.

Schabes, Y. 1991. "Polynomial Time and Space Shift-Reduce Parsing of Arbitrary Context-free Grammars", *Proceedings ACL'91*, Berkeley, Ca.

Schabes, Y. 1992. "Stochastic Lexicalized Tree-Adjoining Grammars", *Proceedings COLING'92*, Nantes, France.

Schabes, Y., M. Roth and R. Osborne, 1993. "Parsing the Wall Street Journal with the Inside-Outside Algorithm", *Proceedings EACL'93*, Utrecht, The Netherlands.

Schabes, Y. and R. Waters, 1996. "Stochastic Lexicalized Tree-Insertion Grammar". In H. Bunt and M. Tomita (eds.) *Recent Advances in Parsing Technology*. Kluwer Academic Publishers.

Scholtes, J. 1992a. "Neural Data-Oriented Parsing (DOP)", *Proceedings of the SHOE Workshop*, Tilburg, The Netherlands.

Scholtes, J. 1992b. "Resolving Linguistic Ambiguities with a Neural Data-Oriented Parsing (DOP) System", in I. Aleksander and J. Taylor (eds.), *Artificial Neural Networks 2*, Vol. 2, Elsevier Science Publishers.

Scholtes, J. and S. Bloembergen, 1992a. "The Design of a Neural Data-Oriented Parsing (DOP) System", *Proceedings of the International Joint Conference on Neural Networks*, (IJCNN), Baltimore, MD.

Scholtes, J. and S. Bloembergen, 1992b. "Corpus Based Parsing with a Self-Organizing Neural Net", *Proceedings of the International Joint Conference on Neural Networks*, (IJCNN), Bejing, China.

Scholtes, J. 1993. *Neural Networks in Natural Language Processing and Information Retrieval*, Ph.D. thesis, Department of Computational Linguistics, University of Amsterdam, The Netherlands.

Schütz, S. 1996. *Part-of-Speech Tagging: Rule-Based, Markovian, Data-Oriented*. Master's Thesis, University of Amsterdam, The Netherlands.

Sekine, S. and R. Grishman, 1995. "A Corpus-based Probabilistic Grammar with Only Two Non-terminals", *Proceedings Fourth International Workshop on Parsing Technologies*, Prague, Czech Republic.

Sima'an, K., R. Bod, S. Krauwer and R. Scha, 1994. "Efficient Disambiguation by means of Stochastic Tree Substitution Grammars", *Proceedings International Conference on New Methods in Language Processing*, UMIST, Manchester, UK.

Sima'an, K. 1995. "An optimized algorithm for Data Oriented Parsing", *Proceedings International Conference on Recent Advances in Natural Language Processing*, Tzigov Chark, Bulgaria.

Sima'an, K. 1996a. "An optimized algorithm for Data Oriented Parsing", in: R. Mitkov and N. Nicolov (eds.), *Recent Advances in Natural Language Processing 1995*, volume 136 of *Current Issues in Linguistic Theory*. John Benjamins, Amsterdam.

Sima'an, K. 1996b. "Computational Complexity of Probabilistic Disambiguation by means of Tree Grammars", *Proceedings COLING-96*, Copenhagen, Denmark.

Sima'an, K. 1997a. "Explanation-Based Learning of Data-Oriented Parsing", in T. Ellison (ed.) *CoNLL97: Computational Natural Language Learning*, ACL'97, Madrid, Spain.

Sima'an, K. 1997b. "Explanation-Based Learning of Partial-Parsing", *Proceedings Workshop on Empirical Learning of Natural Language Tasks, European Conference on Machine Learning 1997*, Prague, Czech Republic.

Simmons, R. and Y. Yu, 1992. "The Acquisition and Use of Context-Dependent Grammars for English", *Computational Linguistics* 18(4), 391-418.

Smith, R. 1973. *Probabilistic Performance Models of Language*, Mouton, The Hague.

Srinivas, B. and A. Joshi, 1995. "Some novel applications of explanation-based learning to parsing lexicalized tree-adjoining grammars", *Proceedings ACL'95*, Cambridge, Mass.

Stolcke, A. 1995. "An efficient probabilistic context-free parsing algorithm that computes prefix probabilities", *Computational Linguistics* 21(2), 165-202.

Suppes, P. 1970. "Probabilistic Grammars for Natural Languages", *Synthese* 22.

Tanenhaus, M. and J. Trueswell, 1995. "Sentence Comprehension", in Miller et al. (eds), *Speech, Language and Communication*, Academic Press.

Tugwell, D. 1995. "A State-Transition Grammar for Data-Oriented Parsing", *Proceedings European Chapter of the ACL'95*, Dublin, Ireland.

Vallduvi, E. 1990. *The Informational Component*. Ph.D. thesis, University of Pennsylvania, PA.

Veldhuijzen van Zanten, G. 1996. *Semantics of update expressions*. Technical Report 24. NWO Priority Programme Language and Speech Technology, The Hague.

Viterbi, A. 1967. "Error bounds for convolutional codes and an asymptotically optimum decoding algorithm", *IEEE Trans. Information Theory*, IT-13, 260-269.

Weischedel, R., M. Meteer, R, Schwarz, L. Ramshaw and J. Palmucci, 1993. "Coping with Ambiguity and Unknown Words through Probabilistic Models", *Computational Linguistics*, 19(2), 359-382.

Wetherell, C. 1980. "Probabilistic Languages: A Review and Some Open Questions", *Computing Surveys*, 12(4).

Winograd, T. 1983. *Language as a Cognitive Process. Volume I: syntax*. Reading, Mass.

Wright, J., E. Wrigley and R. Sharman, 1991. "Adaptive Probabilistic Generalized LR Parsing", *Proceedings Second International Workshop on Parsing Technologies*, Cancun, Mexico.

Zaanen, M. van, 1997. *Error Correction using DOP*. Master's thesis, Department of Computer Science, Vrije Universiteit, The Netherlands.

Zavrel, J. 1996. *Lexical Space: Learning and Using Continuous Linguistic Representations*. Master's Thesis, Department of Philosophy, Utrecht University, The Netherlands.

Zipf, G. 1935. *The Psycho-Biology of Language*, Houghton Mifflin.

Index

Loomis 2
loss of information 110
MacDonald 2; 3; 50
Magerman xi; xiii; 10; 85
Marcus 7; 51; 66
Martin 2
maximum constituent parse 49; 66
Maxwell xiii
Mehler 3
Memory Based Learning 67
memory limitations 109
Mercer 4
metalinguistic judgments 134
Meyer 45
Miller 115
mismatch method 82; 83; 87
Mitchell 3
Montague Grammar 105
Monte Carlo 45-50; 66; 88; 118; 143
Motwani 45
Nadas 85
neurobiology 50
Non-head Property 65
non-head words 58-64; 124
non-standard quantifier scope 104;
    115
Nonbranching Dominance 127
Noord, van 113; 121; 122
number (dis)agreement 78
off-line sampling 136
once-occurring subtrees 124
Oostdijk 7
open-class words 80; 89
Optimality Theory 68
overgeneration 3; 113
Overlap Property 64
overlapping fragments 53
OVIS 112-124
parallelism 109
parse forest 40
part-of-speech tagging 66; 83; 85
partial annotations 104; 105

partial parse method 70; 77; 80
Patil 2
Pearlmutter 3
Penn Treebank 51; 66
Pereira xiii; 9; 66; 85
performance model 1; 2; 109
performance phenomena 4
Peters xiii
Pierrehumbert xi; xiii; 68
platitudes 4
Polanyi xiii; 110
precision 10; 123
preference for mismatches with
    open-class words 89
preference for parses constructed by
    a minimal number of
    mismatches 89
preference for parses that can be
    constructed out of the largest
    possible fragments 22; 92
preference for the most specific
    representation 142
primacy effect 142
Prince 68
Principle of Compositionality of
    Meaning 107; 115
probability of a derivation 19; 27;
    88; 108; 117; 135
probability of a meaning 108; 117
probability of a parse tree 19; 88;
    108; 117
probability of a string 27; 88
probability of a subtree 16-17; 107;
    117
probability of a representation 134
project and integrate method 70
Properness 25
Proust 110n
pseudo-attachments 51
Puckett 3
Raghavan 45
Rajman xi; xiii; 48